"Lynne Finney's heart has poured forth another fine healing tool as it was guided through her keen vision of the restoration that is called for. She shares the path of healing that is the legacy to anyone seeking "the gift in the wound." It is a great deal more than just the pearl in the oyster, it is the ocean out of which both were composed. It is the heart of being awakening from the dreams and nightmares of the past into the profound illuminations of the present."

—Stephen and Ondrea Levine, authors of *Embracing the Beloved*

"The title says it all. Can there be anything more important than learning how to release the past so that freedom and the present and future can become one?"

—Gerald G. Jampolsky, M.D., author of *Love Is Letting Go of Fear*

CLEAR YOUR PAST

Change Your Future

Lynne D. Finney, J.D., M.S.W.

New Harbinger Publications

Publisher's Note

This publication is designed to provide accurate and authoritative information in regard to the subject matter covered. It is sold with the understanding that the publisher is not engaged in rendering psychological, financial, legal, or other professional services. If expert assistance or counseling is needed, the services of a competent professional should be sought.

Distributed in the U.S.A. by Publishers Group West; in Canada by Raincoast Books; in Great Britain by Airlift Book Company, Ltd.; in South Africa by Real Books, Ltd.; in Australia by Boobook; and in New Zealand by Tandem Press.

Copyright © 1997 Lynne D. Finney
New Harbinger Publications, Inc.
5674 Shattuck Avenue
Oakland, CA 94609

Cover design and illustration ©1997 by Lightbourne Images
Text Design by Michele Waters.

Library of Congress Catalog Card Number: 97-66080
ISBN 1-57224-088-1 Paperback

All rights reserved.

Printed in the United States on recycled paper.

New Harbinger Publications' Web site address: www.newharbinger.com

First Printing

With love and gratitude to Rosemary Murray and G. Hugh Allred who helped me clear my past and never wavered in their unconditional love and acceptance.

Table of Contents

Acknowledgments

I am grateful to so many people for enhancing this book and my life that it is impossible to list them all. My family, friends, therapists, clients, colleagues, and readers have all made significant contributions to my growth and healing, as well as to my understanding and refinement of the inner Exploration Process. Clearing my past has made me aware of the constant support and love surrounding me, and has blessed me with the newly found gift of overwhelming gratitude.

Although my parents have passed on, I want to express my gratitude for the love and the strengths they gave me, and for providing a model for endurance and inner healing. I an especially grateful for the love and support of my stepfather, Dale Eunson, who encouraged me to continue writing, and for the brother I love very much.

My heartfelt thanks to Diane Gill, a caring friend, and one of the best and most sensitive therapists I know, for her help in my healing process and her suggestions for this book. I have no words to express my thanks and love to the special friends who cared about me over the years, even when I made it difficult, and taught me the meaning of love: Bill Estell, a courageous and loving spirit who has worked very hard to clear his past; Jacqueline Nelson, who brings joy to the world and is wise beyond her years; Jim and "Pop" Kennicott; Camille Macalou; Karen Perkins; Dagny Andreassen; the Brussow family; Bob and Veda Charrow;

Sandra and Jerry Philpott; Suzanne Merrill; Marcia Harrow; Pierre Terrier; Joan Borysenko; David Schell; Kathy DeWitt, Daisy Fields, Robin and Marcia Frederick, Constance Fairbanks, and Louise Bown—and my dog, Mischka, who is the personification of unconditional love. Special thanks to my friends in our Journey Group—Holly Carlin, Maria Erali, Medford Leake, Becky Leonard, Wendy Welborn, and Susan Wymer, and to my many friends in the Park City Community Church who taught me how caring people are. And much gratitude to the gifted healers who have helped me find inner peace: Nancy Foster, Alan E. Jeppson; Kory Branham; John Nuslein, and Steve and Linda Winget.

I am also grateful for the dedication and pioneering psychological research of Bessel van der Kolk, M.D.; Judith Herman, M.D., Milton Erickson, M.D., Ernest Rossi, Ph.D., and many others who have shed light on the inner workings of our minds, making it easier for all of us to heal.

Last, but not least, I want to thank Kristin Beck for her contributions and encouragement; Farrin Jacobs, my tough and talented editor, for improving my writing with kindness and patience; Kirk Johnson and Gayle Zanca for their talents and care; and all of the people at New Harbinger who made the publishing process enjoyable.

Prologue

The mind of man is capable of of everything because everything is in it,
all the past and all the future.

—Joseph Conrad

Congratulations! Since you are reading this book, you are already well on your way to solving your problems. You recognize that help is available and value yourself enough to reach out for ways to improve your life. You have already taken the most difficult step toward healing by assuming responsibility for your life and making healing a priority.

You have the ability to heal your mind, no matter what has been done to you or what you have done. You have the power to change the old patterns, attitudes, feelings, and behaviors that are restricting your happiness. You can clear your past and create a new future for yourself.

The exercises and techniques in this book have been proven effective in psychotherapy and are used by therapists to help clients with all kinds of problems, such as unsatisfactory relationships, depression, addiction, loss, anxiety attacks, obesity, pain, and even physical ailments. These techniques are the ones I used to heal myself from the effects of severe childhood physical and sexual abuse. For more than ten years, I collected techniques from hundreds of books and therapists and tested them on myself and my clients. My goal was to find the ones that people could use successfully by themselves. I selected and refined the most effective methods—the ones that produced permanent changes—to include in this book.

When we were children, we acquired many beliefs based on misunderstandings about events and our role in them. These childhood misconceptions can limit our options as adults and compel us to act in self-destructive ways, ruining our chances for happiness. By uncovering these erroneous beliefs, many of which are subconscious, we can eliminate them and live fulfilling lives.

One of the most significant advances in the psychological field has been the discovery of the negative effects childhood trauma can have on our feelings, beliefs, and behavior. The latest psychological and neurobiological research shows that there are reasons for self-defeating behavior and harmful repetitive patterns in our lives, and these reasons are usually painful experiences in our pasts. The good news is that we have the ability to clear out these old feelings, behaviors, and patterns by becoming aware of the events that created them and by releasing the old emotions that are still stored in our minds and bodies.

The past determines the present. If you want to change your future, you must clear your past.

The Inner Exploration Process, which you will learn about in the first part of this book, is a tool for exploring your own mind so you can discover the reasons for your behaviors and clear your past. Once you understand your past experiences, you can use your own powerful mental ability to change beliefs that may no longer serve you. You will discover that your mind knows how to heal itself and has all the answers you need.

I know from personal experience that it can be scary facing painful events from the past—events we often have long forgotten. Recovering memories of the sexual abuse I experienced as a child was far from pleasant. I wrote about my recovery and those of other people in my first book, Reach for the Rainbow: Advanced Healing for Survivors of Sexual Abuse. Even though it was distressing to face the fact that my father had abused me, the results of clearing out my old emotions and self-defeating beliefs were well worth the effort. My life and relationships changed dramatically and, after releasing old feelings of rage and hatred, I was able to forgive my parents and become closer to members of my family. I still use the Inner Exploration Process to clear out remaining negative beliefs and behaviors.

Although I uncovered my first memories of abuse in therapy, I used the Inner Exploration Process to do much of the work on my own. As the worst memories were coming out I used the Process with a therapist I needed someone who could reassure me and help me release deeper emotions. Since then, I have refined the Process to help my own clients use it and have also trained thousands of people—including therapists—to use this Process.

Ten years ago I never would have believed how greatly my childhood experiences dominated my adult life. However, my world has changed so dramatically and I am so much more at peace that I can no longer doubt the powerful benefits of clearing my past.

Over the years, as I tested and refined the Inner Exploration Process, I found that it could be used effectively to treat many different kinds of subconscious feelings and beliefs, as well as physical conditions. Most important, I saw clearly that the mind has infinite power, that the human spirit is incredibly resilient, and that people have the ability to heal no matter what they have suffered. I have seen victims of the most terrible child abuse, perpetrators of that abuse, and murderers release the pain of their pasts and heal. I am convinced all mental problems can be healed.

In addition to the Inner Exploration Process, this book contains techniques for a variety of problems and greater self-understanding. You do not need to do all of the exercises. Trust your instincts and start with the ones you feel you need the most or find the most comfortable. Or you may want to try some of them if you are stuck at some point in the Inner Exploration Process. Use what works for you.

We are all our own therapists. Our minds are immensely powerful and know how to protect and heal us. At times we may need help, but if we learn to listen inside, the answers are there. These days psychotherapy is becoming prohibitively expensive, and shortsighted health insurance companies are cutting mental health coverage, putting therapy out of most people's reach. The good news is that we all have the ability to explore our own minds and clear out the limitations caused by past experiences. People have been doing it for generations.

Professional therapists are simply guides who can provide helpful information and support you—no small gift, but as the best therapists acknowledge, each of us is responsible for our own healing. I saw this in my clinical practice as a therapist: When my clients were stuck, I would ask them what they needed to do next. Often they would say they didn't know, looking to me for the answers because I was the therapist. At times I would make suggestions, but other times I would ask them to guess what they needed to do next. They would come up with the perfect solution.

Although you can do much of your own healing, remember that there are over four billion people on Earth and we can help each other. You do not have to do it all alone, and, in fact, it may not be healthy to do so. Life requires balance, and while one part of the equation is accepting responsibility for your own healing, the other part is learning how to ask for and accept help.

There are times when healing can be easier and faster with the help of a support group or a professional. If you are very depressed for more than a couple of weeks, feel that you do not want to live, are addicted to drugs or alcohol, are being abused or are abusing someone, or feel overwhelmed by your emotions or problems, you need to find a therapist to help you. And if you uncover particularly painful memories, you may need the support of a therapist while you deal with them. All of the techniques in this book are used by therapists and you can use them with a therapist or as an adjunct to therapy to help you make faster progress.

Some people have been abused and systematically brainwashed in sadistic, ritualistic cults. If you suspect that you may have been abused in a cult or brainwashed, or if you become very frightened when you used the Inner Exploration Process or any other technique, you need to consult a therapist who is experienced in handling cases of severe abuse.

There are an infinite number of ways to heal—and there is no right or wrong way. We all have our own paths, and heal at our own rates. If these techniques are not right for you, others will be. Keep searching; you will be led to something that works for you. Trust your instincts, your feelings, and the gentle inner voice most of us so often ignore.

During my own healing journey, I tried many techniques, many therapists, many religions, and many self-help books. I took what worked for me and left the rest. I learned to trust my own healing process, and looking back I now realize that, in spite of all my doubts, my process was right for me; I learned something valuable from everything I studied. Trust your own process and your own feelings of what is right for you.

You can make your progress easier by eliminating one common misconception: Most of us believe that life and learning have to be hard. This is a cultural myth. Personal growth is an ongoing journey that may at times be challenging, but it can also be interesting, easy—and even fun. Your expectations determine your experience. I wish someone had told me this fact earlier in my healing journey. As soon as I started telling myself that healing could be easy, it became much easier. Tell yourself right now that healing can be easy and fun, an exciting voyage of discovery, and keep repeating this truth until you believe it.

My wish for you is that you will explore your mind, clear out the limitations from your past, and come to know your true self. Under all the layers of hurt and pain, you will find the real you and discover the infinite power of your mind.

During a time more primitive and cruel than ours, the Buddha said: "If you search the wide world over, you will never find anyone more deserving of love than yourself." That statement is true for you.

Be gentle with yourself.

Part I

The Inner Exploration Process

1

The Power of Your Mind

There is a basic law that like attracts like. That which you mentally project reproduces in kind and negative thoughts definitely attract negative results. Conversely, if a person thinks optimistically and hopefully, he activates life around him positively and thereby attracts to himself positive results. His positive thinking sets in motion creative forces, and success instead of eluding him flows toward him.

—Norman Vincent Peale

Throughout the ages, people have explored the mysteries of their minds using a variety of methods such as meditation, prayer, and more psychological techniques. Experience and science have greatly increased our knowledge of how to heal our minds, and therapeutic techniques have been refined enough to be easily understood and used by most people. Today's psychotherapy is far more effective than older methods in helping us to know ourselves, by revealing the subconscious feelings, memories, and patterns that keep us from using the infinite power of our minds and experiencing happiness.

How Past Experiences Affect You Now

Some people say we only use 3 to 15 percent of our minds. That's like saying your mind is a huge hotel but you only use three or four of the rooms. Nature creates new capacities for immediate needs, not to anticipate possible future circumstances. Scientists studying the course of evolution discovered that animals survived by adapting to new conditions and that their brain capacity and other functions grew to meet new challenges. It is closer to the truth to say that you only use 3 to 15 percent of your brain consciously; most of your brain functions outside of your conscious awareness, and scientists have only begun to understand its infinite power.

Our heads contain a bio-computer more complex than any electronic computer yet devised. According to neurobiologists, our brains are made up of more than ten billion neurons that analyze, interpret, compare, associate, store, and transmit information from the world around us. The conscious part of our minds is unable to process all of this input; it can only deal with information from one or two senses at a time. But our subconscious handles millions of bits of information every second, even though we are not consciously aware of this activity. Your subconscious is constantly recording all of our experiences, thoughts, and emotions, and this input becomes the program that determines your reactions and behavior.

How we react to present events is determined by the information stored in our brains from all of our past experiences. This information is imprinted in the enormous subconscious part of our minds and is the mental software that causes us to select and focus on certain events in the present. Out of a number of possibilities, our minds tend to focus only on those events that are consistent with our earlier experiences and our conscious and unconscious beliefs and intentions. Our minds ignore other events that may be occurring at the same instant. Our past experiences and old beliefs make up the mental program that "creates our reality" by selecting what we sense and experience.

One aspect of enlightenment is learning to use the subconscious part of our minds consciously by uncovering the flaws in our mental programs so that we can make choices with awareness. The more conscious we are of our how our minds work, the more power we have to make our lives the way we want them to be.

Our minds have limitless power—power we have only begun to harness. But, as long as we are not aware of what makes us act the way we do, we are allowing ourselves to be controlled by painful events from our pasts. We think we are free, but most of us are controlled like puppets, blindly reacting to old wounds and childhood misconceptions. We may believe we act with a great deal of deliberation and thoughtful planning, but the truth is that our lives may be governed by our preconditioning. This preconditioning is the mental programming instilled in us as children by events that were traumatic to us, because, as children, we were unable to analyze and assimilate painful experiences. Until you become aware of the secrets your mind holds, you may be trapped in recurring patterns of behavior and limited by old beliefs, emotions, and decisions buried in your subconscious.

Far too many people believe that their emotions control them, that other people make them angry, or that feelings of depression arise out of nowhere. This is not the case. Anger is a personal reaction, an individual interpretation of present circumstances based on prior experiences; other people might not become angry under the same circumstances. And no one can catch depression like a cold. There is a reason for depression, although it may be subconscious.

Psychotherapy helps people uncover their unconscious limitations, attitudes, and beliefs so they can analyze them consciously and choose healthier ones. The good news is that you can use therapeutic techniques yourself and explore your own mind, without going to a therapist. Long before there were licensed therapists, people successfully healed themselves through self-analysis by exploring their minds and thoughts. In fact, some of the techniques in this book have been used by spiritual teachers for thousands of years and are now being rediscovered and adapted by therapists.

Most spiritual teachers recognize the reality of how past experiences affect us, counseling us to clear our pasts and learn to know our true selves: the innocent, loving child who lives inside us all. Ancient Hindu scriptures and recent books such as *The Celestine Prophecy* teach that we must peel away old layers of falsehood, misconception, and pain in order to reach enlightenment.

Spirituality and psychology are inextricably intertwined; the mind is the key to both, and both involve clearing out false beliefs. Spiritual realization doesn't require adding anything to what you already are, but it demands that you strip away the false beliefs that prevent you from seeing your true self and the miracles around you. Spiritual exploration and psychological healing are both paths on the same journey to self-awareness. Both teach that the secret to freedom is inside your own mind. Awareness will set you free. You have choices only when you are consciously aware of what you are doing and why.

You Can Change Your Personality

Misconceptions abound about how the human mind works and why people act the way they do. Some people believe they were born with a certain personality that can't be changed: "That's just the way I am." The truth is that you can change any facet of your personality or behavior. What you think of as your "personality" is not an immutable set of characteristics. Rather, it is a set of reaction patterns shaped by past responses to painful events. Once these patterns are established in your brain, you repeat them automatically when presented with situations that are similar to past events. But these patterns can be changed.

A child who loses a parent to death or abandonment may develop an intense fear of abandonment and as an adult may not be able to form intimate relationships for fear of losing loved ones. Or, that person may experience a pattern of relationships where he or she is abandoned.

We learn from experience. If an infant is given a toy ball and told it is a ball, that infant will eventually begin to associate roundness with the word "ball" and call all round objects, such as oranges, "balls." But, once a child tastes an orange, new information is added through this experience. The child's mind will begin to differentiate between a toy ball and an orange. However, an event such as the loss or abandonment of a parent is so painful that information about this event is sent to a subconcious part of the brain that is isolated and does not receive new information. If the child concludes that loved ones will leave, or that the child is responsible and unlovable, those subconcious beliefs remain unchanged no matter how often the child may be told otherwise later in life. When the child begins to feel love as an adult, feelings of love are associated with the lost parent, triggering old feelings and old beliefs. We are able to add new information and adjust our beliefs consciously if the basic information is conscious. But our old beliefs are subconscious, the new information will not reach them. Old beliefs will continue to control our reactions.

When the child grows up, he or she does not deliberately choose partners who will leave, but instead is subconsciously drawn to people who will do so. Unconscious fear may create behaviors, such as possessiveness or provoking fights, that cause people to leave. It is often easier and more comfortable to see such situations as someone else's fault, but the hard truth is that people often unconsciously bring these events on themselves. This is usually the case if these situations occur more than once, forming a pattern.

Even when a pattern is painful and destructive, we continue to repeat it because that pattern is imprinted in our brain and feels familiar. When presented with change, we feel uncomfortable, insecure, and frightened and therefore tend to remain in our dysfunctional patterns. We keep repeating these patterns, finding ourselves unconsciously drawn to events that confirm our past history, until our lives become so painful that we are forced to face what is inside our minds.

But you don't have to wait to hit bottom. You can learn to consciously control your actions and reactions by uncovering your unconscious beliefs and using effective psychological techniques to heal yourself. One of the hardest lessons for me during my recovery from childhood abuse was to accept the fact that I am responsible for my life now. I was the quintessential victim; I saw everything that happened to me as someone else's fault. I felt powerless, wronged, betrayed, battered by fate. My therapist had a poster in her office that said: "Baby, you are the only problem you will ever have, and you are the only solution." I hated that poster and vigorously resisted my therapist's efforts to help me see that, although I was abused as a child, no one was abusing me now—except me. Accepting the possibility that I might be responsible for my present circumstances and that I had the ability to change them was a major breakthrough for me.

How Your Past Limits You

We would like to believe we can just forget unpleasant past events, but the results of recent psychological studies indicate that we have to resolve them in order to put them behind us. Psychologists studying veterans of the Korean Conflict and the Vietnam War observed that soldiers subjected to bloody combat or tortured as prisoners of war displayed a cluster of similar symptoms, including loss of memory of the traumatic incidents, inappropriate anger, nightmares, insomnia, depression, flashbacks, and alienation from others. The most significant symptom was that these soldiers suffered from amnesia—they had no conscious memory of their traumatic experiences. After the soldiers received therapy to help recover the repressed memories of the traumatic experiences, release the intense emotions, and resolve the guilt surrounding the experiences, their symptoms disappeared.

Similar symptoms, including amnesia, were found to exist in victims of natural disasters and violent crimes. Since these symptoms resulted from traumatic experiences, the syndrome was labeled *post-traumatic stress disorder.* This syndrome has been recognized by the psychiatric profession in the United States and Europe since World War II. Post-traumatic stress disorder has also been found in children who have been abused or subjected to other types of trauma.

Neurobiological studies at Harvard Medical School provide new insights into post-traumatic stress disorder and how the human mind establishes repetitive patterns that govern future behavior. Neurobiologists have isolated some of the brain functions responsible for imprinting a traumatic event in the subconscious while simultaneously blocking that event from the conscious mind. Groundbreaking research by psychiatrists at Harvard Medical School and other institutions indicates that intense emotions interfere with information processing, leading to amnesia.

These studies also show that the more suppressed memories people bring to consciousness, the more they heal. This fact was discovered during the studies of combat veterans in World War II and in later studies of veterans of Korea and Vietnam who were being treated for post-traumatic stress disorder. These conclusions have been recently confirmed by neuroradiological studies on trauma conducted by Bessel van der Kolk, M.D., a world-renowned psychiatrist on the faculty of Harvard Medical School and one of the foremost experts on trauma and memory, and researchers at other institutions around the world. Dr. van der Kolk used Positron Emission Tomography (PET) technology, a variation on the CAT scan, to map areas of trauma in people's brains. He found that, as the repressed trauma was released, the areas of trauma decrease in size. He also discovered that the more amnesia people have, the more symptomatic they are, and concluded that people who retrieve all of their memories do much better than people who still have repressed memories.

Living with unresolved traumatic memories is at best an exhausting struggle and at worst a seemingly unending nightmare. Repressed trauma is responsible for an enormous variety of problems, including depression, unhealthy relationships, feelings of alienation, explosive anger, self-sabotage, and the inability to experience joy or love. When childhood trauma is particularly severe, such as in cases of physical and sexual abuse, the effects may include alcohol and drug addiction, eating disorders, revictimization, perpetration of abuse, and a large variety of physical disorders. Most people try many different kinds of therapy and self-help techniques without success before they finally obtain results through techniques such as the Inner Exploration Process described in this book. The Process and similar techniques achieve permanent results more rapidly because they address all of the elements of effective healing: uncovering forgotten painful events and decisions, releasing emotions, changing negative beliefs, and discovering the truth about ourselves.

How Our Brains React to Trauma

Traumatic events are processed by our minds differently than ordinary events. Ordinary events are processed consciously at the time they occur by a part of the brain called the hippocampus. However, this conscious part of the mind is only a tiny part of the whole; the rest, the subconscious, is enormous in comparison.

The conscious part of your mind can only focus on information it perceives through one or two of your senses at any one time. You may be intermittently aware of what you are reading, the temperature of the room, noises around you, or a sensation in your body. But your conscious mind can't focus on all of these things at once. However, your subconscious records all of this information from all of your senses continuously. It contains memories of everything you experience every minute of your life.

At any one moment, the conscious part of your mind focuses on particular information coming from one or two of your senses, analyzes it, and puts it into perspective with other information and beliefs. For example, your eyes are seeing the words on this page and your brain is transmitting the information to your hippocampus so the information can be analyzed in relation to prior beliefs and knowledge you have acquired. Although the analysis usually takes place quickly and mostly unconsciously, you may be aware of thinking: "Yes, that seems to fit with what I have experienced"; or "Hmmm, that's something I never considered before—I need to think about that"; or "That's nonsense!" As you go about your daily activities, your mind is constantly analyzing, judging, and putting the information it receives into perspective based on earlier beliefs and information you have acquired.

This analysis may alter the information you receive in order to conform to your prior beliefs and experiences. That is why ordinary memories, memories of events that were selected as the focus of your conscious mind, may sometimes be distorted when compared to the actual events. When you are asked to recall an event from a normal day, you may have difficulty remembering the details, and different people may remember the same event very differently, depending on what aspects their conscious mind chose to focus on and how their past events and beliefs affect what they experienced.

Have you ever discussed a movie with friends after you watched it together? Did you find that you all remembered different parts and had different interpretations of what happened? You each remembered what was significant to you.

Our minds handle traumatic events—those that evoke overwhelming emotions—differently. Trauma occurs when we are overwhelmed by stress and such intense emotions that adrenaline is released, causing our minds to handle information about the event differently from ordinary events. Trauma is difficult to define because an event that might be stressful and overwhelming to one person might not have the same effect on someone else. Young children are especially prone to traumatic reactions because they do not have the ability to understand many things that happen around them; even loud noises or angry voices may be sufficiently confusing and frightening to an infant to cause a traumatic reaction.

Contrary to the popular belief that infants are unaware of what happens around them, infants interpret many things they hear, and negative statements can become imprinted in their brains. These statements can become part of an infant's personality and affect the person throughout his or her life. There are even cases where adults have recalled hearing the doctors who delivered them say something negative during their births, such as that they were too big and had hurt their mothers. Although an adult would know that being large was not a baby's fault, newborn babies may feel grief and guilt because they believe they are responsible for hurting their mothers. These beliefs may be imprinted in their minds, causing unconscious, lifelong guilt. Another example is a child hearing parents arguing. Overhearing an argument might not be traumatic to an adult, but overhearing the same argument might cause sufficient stress in a young child to cause a traumatic reaction, especially if the child concludes the argument was somehow his or her fault.

The adrenaline that is released due to the strong emotions produced by traumatic events triggers chemical reactions in our brains. Fascinating new research on memory and learning shows that we learn better and remember more when our adrenaline is flowing—when we are under stress. Scientists found that mice injected with adrenaline remembered tasks they learned longer than mice that did not receive adrenaline. Experiments on humans revealed that when people are emotionally involved in experiences and produce adrenaline they learn more from emotional experiences and have better long-term memory of such experiences than people who have no emotional involvement. These findings shed new light on how behavioral patterns are impressed in our minds by stressful situations, causing us to repeat what we learned from them, and why our memories of such situations are more reliable than memories of nonstressful events.

The release of adrenaline and other chemical reactions in our brains causes our minds to bypass the hippocampus, the conscious part of our brains that analyzes what we experience. Extreme stress and intense emotions can overload the processing part of our minds so that we are unable to consciously analyze and process the event. Information about the traumatic event is sent directly to another part of our brains, a more ancient part that handles emotions. Here the experience is recorded exactly as it occurs, including all of the information received from our five senses and all of the intense emotions the experience may evoke. Traumatic events are not consciously evaluated or put into perspective because they are not analyzed by the conscious processing part of our brains. Traumatic memories are imprinted subconsciously in our minds just as they were experienced, even though the events may be blocked from our conscious awareness.

Even though we may not consciously remember the traumatic events or the intense emotions we felt at the time, the memories and emotions remain trapped in our minds and bodies. The emotions, along with the sights, sounds, smells, tastes, and body sensations, are indelibly recorded in subconscious parts of our minds, frozen just as the event occurred, unprocessed and unresolved. Dr. van der Kolk describes these traumatic memories as being like mummies sealed in sarcophagi and buried underground. As long as no air can get inside these coffins, the bodies remain in the condition they were in when they were buried. Like mummies, unrecovered memories do not change. They are uncontaminated when first uncovered because no other information has reached them.

When first recovered, repressed memories are usually accurate because they are pristine, untainted by conscious processing. Therefore, traumatic memories that have been blocked from consciousness are far more reliable than ordinary memories, as has been shown in studies where blocked memories were corroborated by witnesses and other evidence. When these traumatic memories are brought to consciousness, they are more detailed and precise than ordinary memories because they have never been altered through analysis. You will be astonished at the details you are able to remember as you uncover events from your past.

These groundbreaking neurobiological discoveries reveal that as long as we have unprocessed trauma in our minds, we may not have control over our emotions or behavior in certain situations. When suppressed memories are triggered, the analytical part of our brain may be bypassed, leaving us without the ability to reason or judge our actions. Our responses are then determined by subconcious memories and emotions stored in our brains. The implications of these physiological findings are staggering and will require a reevaluation of our beliefs about criminal responsibility, punishment versus healing, and even concepts of free will. Even more important, however, these breakthroughs have shown us how to devise psychological techniques that achieve more effective, rapid, and permanent results. We now have the ability to cure the underlying causes of psychological problems by bringing the repressed memories, emotions and beliefs to consciousness.

Childhood Beliefs Affect Your Future

Children are likely to experience symptoms of post-traumatic stress from a variety of events, many of which might not seem traumatic to an adult but can be confusing and overwhelming to a child. When children experience distressing events, such as a death in the family, abandonment, abuse, or even being yelled at, they cannot understand what is happening; their minds are engulfed by powerful emotions that overwhelm the processing part of the brain, which becomes unable to cope with the flood of emotions and is bypassed. Information about the traumatic event is shunted to the subconscious, where the memory and emotions are imprinted but blocked from conscious awareness.

When a child is severely distressed and confused, memories of that portion of the child's life may be suppressed and become frozen in time. When those memories are recovered, the person will experience the events as though he or she were still at the age when the events occurred. A fifty-year-old man may experience the feelings and thoughts he had as a four-year-old when he heard his parents fighting. He may even begin to talk like a four-year-old. When you recover repressed memories, you may experience the events as though they were occurring in the present. You may relive the intense emotions you shut off at the time, although any physical pain you may have suffered is far less.

The younger a child is, the less able he or she is to understand and cope. It is therefore more likely that a traumatic event the child experiences will be repressed—and misunderstood. These misunderstandings are usually negative conclusions about being responsible in some way for the event and thus being "bad." Or the misunderstanding can be destructive decisions about other people and the universe. These unconscious beliefs create self-defeating attitudes and patterns of behavior that continue into adulthood, destroying a person's ability to experience happiness until the beliefs are resolved.

One of my clients, whom I will call Julie, grew up in a family of eight children. She recalled with a great deal of pain how as a small child she wanted desperately to be closer to her busy and rather distant mother. When she was five, Julie thought long and hard about what she could do to win her mother's approval and love. Her mother collected pictures of horses, so Julie spent weeks in kindergarten laboriously drawing a picture of a horse. When Julie finished the picture, she ran home to give it to her mother, but her mother was on the phone and pushed her away without looking at the drawing.

Julie was devastated by feelings of rejection, anger, disappointment, failure, and grief—feelings so overwhelming that she blocked them from her conscious memory. When she recovered those feelings, Julie found that as a child she had concluded from this incident that her mother would never love her. In fact, she had decided that no one would ever love her, that she was inherently unlovable, and that it was not worth working hard or planning anything because whatever she did would not be appreciated. As a result, her life had been controlled by these beliefs for almost thirty years.

These core beliefs destroyed Julie's relationships and kept her from completing goals such as obtaining a college degree. Once she recovered the memories and released the pain she felt when her mother pushed her away, Julie realized that her childhood decisions were erroneous and she was able to view her mother's actions from a more adult and realistic perspective. Julie understood that her mother's actions did not mean she did not love her, but simply that her mother was under so much stress from raising eight children that she was too exhausted to fulfill Julie's emotional needs. After Julie realized that nothing was wrong with her, she blossomed almost immediately. She took charge of her life, reconciled with her husband, and finished college.

Like Julie, children who are traumatized repress their memories longer than adults who suffer trauma, and many do not recover the memories until their thirties or forties. As adults, people may have totally forgotten the emotional or physical trauma they suffered as children, but they start therapy because they are having nightmares or flashbacks of events they do not recall, or because they are depressed, angry, or caught in patterns of victimization. Their subconscious somehow knows when they are mature enough to process the memories consciously and it sends them signals that they need to clear their pasts.

How Memories Are Repressed

Memories can be repressed in various ways. Some people block out both the painful event and the emotions surrounding it. Others remember details of the event, but suppress the feelings they had. Those who block only the emotions are often harder to treat because they insistently deny that the events harmed them, assuming that, since they have no feelings, the event did not affect them. Unfortunately, the opposite is true. Suppressed emotions can establish destructive unconscious behavioral patterns that wreak havoc on our adult lives even if we consciously remember what occurred. This is because these old emotions can be triggered by present events, causing us to overreact and automatically repeat harmful patterns of behavior.

Children who are repeatedly abused over long periods of time have different methods of coping. Some may block out whole years of their childhood, as I did. These children create ego states, parts of their minds that hold the memories. And some children are so severely abused that they survive not only by blocking memories of the abuse from their conscious minds, but by creating a number of new, distinct personalities to deal with their abusers. This coping mechanism, which used to be known as multiple personality disorder and is now called dissociative identity disorder, affects many more people than therapists previously recognized.

Body Memories

Scientists have found that we store traumatic memories not only in our minds but in our bodies as well. In fact, neurobiologists have discovered that brain functions are not confined to our heads. Neuropeptides and neurotransmitters, the mechanisms that send information to various parts of the brain, are found in other parts of the body including the stomach, a discovery that seems to validate the theory of "gut" instincts and reactions.

Your body is a natural lie detector. It not only stores information and emotions, but gives you feedback and warnings through bodily sensations. These sensations can be more reliable than thoughts. When you feel tension or discomfort in your body, you are receiving a signal that something is wrong or false. When there is truth, you feel peace. How many times have you been in a situation where your body felt uncomfortable and you felt as though you wanted to get away, but your mind said you should stay or that you should be nice to the person or be tolerant, and the consequences were disastrous? By learning to tune into the signals your body provides, thus becoming more aware of when you feel peace and when you feel discomfort, you can gain greater insight into what is happening around you and avoid harmful situations.

Not only can your body alert you to potential harm, but because it retains memories of stressful situations, your body can suffer from painful events long past. The stress of trauma can create a multitude of physical ailments, such as headaches, heart palpitations, impotence, and gastrointestinal problems. People may experience medically inexplicable body sensations that are related to childhood trauma, such as numbness in the arms if the person was restrained or pain with intercourse if the person was raped. Abuse victims are sometimes diagnosed with somatization disorder, which means they suffer from multiple recurrent physical complaints over a period of years for which no medical cause can be found.

Destructive Childhood Conclusions

One of the most damaging results of repressing traumatic events is that children also suppress the erroneous conclusions they make based on those events—conclusions that affect their view of themselves and their world for the rest of their lives. A common example of such conclusions reached by children is that they are somehow responsible for their own or a loved one's illness, a death in the family, parental divorce, or their own abuse. They may even believe that their angry thoughts can cause damage or kill. Because young children are at an egocentric developmental stage, they believe they are the center of the universe, causing everything that happens to them. Children also quickly learn that they are punished when they are "bad." Since illness or the loss of a loved one or abuse can seem like punishment to a child, children assume that they must be bad, and their self-esteem is destroyed. So if a parent, sibling, abuser or other important person died when you were young, you may have concluded at the time that you were somehow responsible for the death.

Maya Angelou, renowned poet, educator, author, actress, and civil rights activist, described how she concluded as a child that she had killed her abuser: "When I was seven and one-half years of age, I was raped. I told my mother about it and the man responsible was put in jail. For some reason he was released soon afterward and a couple of days later he was found murdered. My child's mind informed me that my voice [as a witness at the trial] had caused his death, and as a result of that belief I didn't speak a word again until I was thirteen."

Obviously the belief that you killed someone would have a devastating effect on your self-esteem, causing guilt and other feelings that could negatively affect your life. If you are forty years old, you might think that the death of a family member or friend when you were five is no longer important, but unfortunately unresolved past losses will make subsequent losses more painful and may affect your present behavior and relationships. The past will continue to haunt you until you deal with it.

Most children's destructive beliefs go one step further: they hear that God protects "good little children" and so conclude that if they are ill, injured, abused, lose a loved one, or suffer other painful events, they must be so bad that even God does not love them and is punishing them. Such beliefs can destroy their self-esteem and implant a frightening view of an unsafe and punitive universe. This negative view of themselves and their universe will destroy their happiness until they become aware of their original erroneous conclusions and change them.

Even incidents that seem innocuous can have far-reaching effects. I have seen a large number of cases where people have been unable to do things or learn certain subjects because a parent, teacher, or older person told them as children that they were stupid. There are many studies demonstrating that girls have traditionally performed less well at math and science than boys because teachers told the girls that they could not learn these subjects. Even though a child may have long forgotten being called stupid or incapable, the subconscious mind remembers and may act on that belief. When the incident and the limiting belief are brought to conscious awareness, most people find that they can learn and do things they could not do before.

Healing the Past

Many people assume that a child will simply "grow out of" problems and that if no one talks about unpleasant experiences, the effects will just go away. Unfortunately, research shows that just the opposite is true. Refusing to talk about frightening events increases the trauma. Healing can take place only if these events are consciously processed and the emotions ventilated. This is why rape crisis programs and other support groups that provide an opportunity for people to express emotions are so successful. The sad truth is that repressed memories and emotions remain frozen, trapped inside us, festering and ruining our lives. The destruction continues until we bring the memories and emotions to conscious awareness where they can be resolved.

When I started my own therapy, I found it hard to accept the fact that events in my early childhood could continue to have such an enormous impact on my life as an adult. I did not want to believe that I was still repeating the painful patterns established in my childhood. I was not convinced until I saw how my life changed after I uncovered and changed self-defeating decisions I had made as a child. Once I became consciously aware of old traumas and beliefs, I was no longer dominated by lifelong destructive patterns of behavior and exaggerated emotional responses.

Most people do not want to believe that their early childhood experiences still have such a profound effect on their behavior. They insist that people cannot blame everything on their parents. While it is true that blaming your parents is unproductive, understanding your reactions to what they did can help you become aware of patterns of behavior that you may want to change—and to take responsibility for them. You may have been abused when you were young, but no one is abusing you now— except yourself. You are responsible for your own actions and healing now.

You may be wondering if all psychological problems are based on responses to traumatic experiences. The vast majority are, according to recent research and clinical experience. There is a reason for dysfunctional behavior; it does not occur at random. We were designed to function perfectly; our minds and bodies are miraculous mechanisms which are constantly working to bring us to a perfect state of mental and physical health. We were born to be happy and loving. If we hurt ourselves or others, there is a reason—and, in the absence of a physical explanation such as a brain tumor or drugs, the reason is likely to be painful unresolved events in our pasts.

Recent studies indicate that even some genetic defects require extreme stress in order to be activated. Many people with a particular genetic defect, such as a tendency toward alcoholism, never exhibit the trait if not subjected to trauma. Scientists call these "two-hit genes" because the genetic tendencies remain latent unless activated by extreme stress. Other studies show that the majority of people who seek therapy have experienced some sort of childhood trauma.

Experiencing how you felt about a childhood episode can help you break out of a lifelong dysfunctional pattern of behavior. For example, Bill, a successful businessman in his fifties, wanted to find out why his relationships were unsatisfactory. His wife and children thought him cold and domineering because he never talked about his feelings or his problems. He would not let his family or his employees help him; he always had to be in control and do everything himself. Bill's inability to share his feelings or rely on others left him isolated, especially after his wife left him.

While Bill was in a relaxed state, I simply asked his mind to take him back to a memory or give him information as to why he would not show his emotions or ask for help. Bill was quiet for a few minutes and then tears started pouring down his cheeks. When I asked him how old he was, he replied: "Four." I asked where he was and he said, in a childish voice, "In a chair, watching my parents leave."

Bill recalled his terror and grief at being left with his infant brother by his parents, who worked in the family hardware store during the Depression. At four years old, he had no sense of time and could not comprehend when his parents would return or if they ever would. He remembered that his aunt looked in on him for a few minutes each afternoon. When his aunt found him crying, she told him that if he cried or complained he would be left all alone forever. She also told him he had to be good and take care of his infant brother and himself if he wanted his parents to return.

As he released his pain and fear, Bill realized that the aunt he had feared as a child had been only fifteen years old herself. Bill saw that his entire life had been organized around his childhood conclusions based on his aunt's admonitions: If you want to be loved and you do not want to be left alone, you must be stoic, never complain or show your feelings, and help others without asking for anything for yourself.

After Bill released his childhood feelings and reevaluated his early beliefs, his new awareness enabled him to get in touch with his feelings and share them with his family, including problems he was having in his business. His family and friends responded warmly when he started asking for their help. Less than three months later, Bill told me, "I feel wonderful about the changes in myself; it's amazing, I feel so good. I enjoy life."

Bill was an intelligent man who had tried using his logic and willpower to break out of his dysfunctional patterns of behavior before coming to therapy. But only after he recalled his childhood trauma, expressed his feelings about being left alone, and reassessed the unconscious decisions he made as a child, was he able to permanently alter his behavior. Most people do not resolve as many problems as Bill by recovering one memory, but each time a suppressed memory is cleared, they gain more freedom.

As Bill found, it is not enough merely to know you have a behavior or belief you want to change. Many dysfunctional core beliefs were imprinted at such an early age and at such a deep, unconscious level that conscious efforts to change the behavior are ineffective. Studies show that talk therapy alone is not effective in making permanent changes in behavior because we cannot talk about what we do not remember. Self-defeating beliefs and behaviors can be altered most effectively when the underlying causes can be brought to consciousness and the suppressed emotions are released.

Unfortunately, most people have some self-defeating beliefs and behaviors resulting from painful and confusing childhood experiences. The good news is that these beliefs and behaviors can be changed. Healing begins when the underlying causes are brought to consciousness and the old emotions are released.

However, healing is not simply a matter of clearing away self-defeating beliefs and behaviors. It is equally important to improve your self-esteem by creating positive beliefs and behaviors. Along with the Inner Exploration Process, this book also provides a variety of techniques to help you recognize your strengths, develop healthy self-esteem, take care of yourself, create a positive view of the world, and learn new behaviors that will help you enjoy your life. Use these exercises to keep a balance between clearing your past and enjoying your life right now.

2

Inner Exploration—A Process for Clearing Your Past

We can take heart when we have reached the darkest point of the journey because we know from the stories of those who have gone before us that the dawn is at hand. And we can have faith that although we may seem to be following a narrow and perilous road alone, it has been tread countless times before. We are not now, nor will we ever be, alone.

—**Joan Borysenko,** *Guilt Is the Teacher, Love Is the Lesson*

The Inner Exploration Process is a method for expanding self-awareness by going inside your mind to unlock its secrets and obtain knowledge about past events you may have forgotten that may be limiting your life now. It will enable you to gain access to the information stored in your subconscious so that you can clear out old emotions and self-defeating beliefs. This is the main technique I use for my own healing, and it is the one my therapy clients found the most helpful. People have used similar techniques for centuries to attain inner peace and enlightenment.

This process is effective because it allows you to focus on any problem, pain, feeling, or belief that troubles you and quickly discover and resolve the underlying cause by simply asking your own mind for an answer. You can also ask your mind to tell you what you need to know right now for your recovery. The Process can help reveal the truth about you, who you *really* are, rather than the lies you believe about yourself. After you use this process for a while, you will find that your mind has all the answers you need to heal any situation.

I strongly urge you to read through all the chapters in part I about the Inner Exploration Process at least once before you try it. When you first start using the Process, you may find it helpful to have the summary on page 37 close at hand to remind you of the steps.

The Process
Choosing an Issue

Most people use the Inner Exploration Process when they have a specific problem or condition they want to resolve, such as an unsatisfactory relationship, unexplained anxiety, or uncontrollable anger. There is no limit to the types of issues and problems that can be explored; they range from very specific issues like why you had a fight with your partner this morning or why you have tension in your neck, to more general problems such as recurring patterns of betrayal or feelings of depression. Any uncomfortable feeling, harmful behavior, or physical symptom is grist for the mill and can be used to find out more about yourself and how you think. The purpose of selecting an issue is so that you can ask your mind for a memory or information that will explain why you feel or act a certain way, or have a particular problem, pain, or disease.

You may find it difficult to believe that events that occurred so long ago could still be affecting you now. However, when you use the Inner Exploration Process to focus on a particular issue, you will see that the memory you recover is directly related to the problem or feelings you have now. After you actually experience the connection between past and present events, you will fully comprehend how greatly the past affects your life now and why it is crucial to clear it out.

Pick the issue that is foremost in your mind right now. You may not think in the overall scheme of things that this issue is the most important, but if it is the focal point of your thoughts at the moment, your mind is highlighting it for you because it is the best one for you to deal with now. You can use the Process as many times as you want, so there is no need to feel anxious about whether the issue you choose is the right one. Whatever issue you select is always the right one. If you continue to have anxiety about selecting the "right" or "perfect" issue, you might use that anxiety as the issue for your session. Why do you have to do everything perfectly? What has made you so afraid of making a mistake?

I have been amazed by how many different problems the Process can resolve and how precise it can be in pinpointing the underlying causes. Years ago, I used the Process almost exclusively for psychological problems and patterns, until one day a client I will call Laura, who had come to therapy to resolve the effects of childhood sexual abuse, complained about her inability to lose weight. Laura weighed over two hundred pounds and the doctors she had consulted were unable to find any physical reason for her obesity. She had tried many diets over the years but lost very little weight, and whatever weight she lost she gained back in a couple of months. Laura wanted to use the Process to find out why she couldn't lose weight. I was skeptical but asked her mind to take her to a memory or information that would explain why she was overweight.

Laura retrieved a vivid memory of being raped by her adoptive father. While she was experiencing the overwhelming feelings of helplessness she felt as a child she recalled thinking how desperately she wanted to be able to protect herself. She wanted to be big and strong like a man so that men would leave her alone. She decided she didn't want to be pretty because she would attract sexual advances. After releasing the pain of this memory, Laura was able to understand that as an adult she could use her intelligence to protect herself and did not have to make herself unattractive. She realized that being overweight would not protect her and might even work against her because she could not run away form a dangerous situation as fast. I was not sure what effect uncovering these childhood decisions would have on Laura and was astonished to watch her lose over fifty pounds in three months *without dieting.* I later used the Process with other overweight or anorexic clients who also uncovered damaging beliefs that led to changes in their eating habits and their weights. In most cases, the beliefs arose from threats or perceived threats to sexual safety, but not necessarily from actual molestation. One woman's decision to become overweight was based on a negative comment make by her mother about the daughter's developing body when she was in puberty.

Some people think their lives are such a mess that they will not be able to select just one issue to use as a focus for the Process. However, it does not matter what issue or problem you choose, or if you even select an issue, because your mind will give you precisely what you need to know anyway. If you cannot choose an issue, simply ask yourself gently: "What do I need to explore right now?" Whatever subsequent thought you have is exactly what you need to focus on in this moment.

If you think of more than one possible issue, select the one you feel most comfortable facing first. Ask your mind to give you information or a memory about the first issue and if no answer arises in your mind, go on to the next. Or ask about both and see what unfolds. There is no right or wrong in this. You will always get what is right for you at the time because your subconscious mind knows everything about you and will give you exactly what you need in order to heal. Your subconscious will also provide the information and memories in the order that is most helpful to you. After a couple of years of using this technique, when I looked back on what I learned, I saw clearly that my subconscious mind had a perfect plan for my healing and always led me exactly where I needed to go. The more you use this process, the more you will discover the incredible knowledge and healing power of your mind.

It is not even necessary to focus on any specific issue. The Inner Exploration Process is a tool for self-exploration, for becoming aware of who you really are and the infinite power of your mind. When you use the Process, you only have to ask your mind for the information that you need right now to learn the truth about yourself, who you really are. Ask your mind to uncover the lies that are keeping you from knowing the truth of who you are. Since your mind knows exactly how to heal you and what you need to work on first, your mind will give you whatever memory or information you need most right now.

Become Receptive through Relaxation

Most of us are so consumed with daily activities, worries about the future, and fears from the past that we never analyze what we are doing or why. We race around, totally unaware of who we are or the power inside us. The only thing preventing us from knowing ourselves is that we do not take the time to relax and explore our minds.

To go inside your mind, you need to become as relaxed as possible. Find a place where you will not be disturbed and where you feel safe and comfortable. It's usually best to sit up and keep your spine straight so your energy will flow freely and you won't fall asleep. However, after I used this process for several months, I could do it lying down and still remain awake. I often did it in bed at night or just after waking up in the morning, when I was already in a relaxed state.

Start by taking deep, slow breaths. Breathe in and allow the air to completely fill your lungs. Breathe from your diaphragm (from your abdomen, not your shoulders) and fill your lungs completely. Feel the air going into your nostrils and down into your lungs. As you exhale, let go of any tension you may feel. Concentrate on your breathing for a couple of minutes, breathing deeply and slowly, feeling the air flowing in and out of your body.

Next I recommend that you use the progressive muscle relaxation exercise on page 149 to reach a deeper state of relaxation, but you may use whatever relaxation techniques work best for you.

To deepen your state of relaxation, visualize walking down some safe, well-lighted stairs. Picture yourself walking down, step by step, until you are very relaxed and feel that you have gone down as far as you need to. Some people prefer to go down in a mental elevator or through a tunnel. Do whatever feels the most comfortable for you.

Tell yourself that you are in control of this process and that you can come out of the state of relaxation at any time you choose. Also tell yourself that you will keep your adult self with you at all times as an observer and that you will remain aware of what you experience. You will be observing yourself and what happens all through this process. You are in control and can stop whenever you want.

If you are distracted by sounds around you, tell yourself that the sounds are safe ones and that they will not disturb you but will simply take you deeper into relaxation.

How to Recover Memories

When you feel very relaxed, gently ask yourself in your mind for information or to show you a memory about the issue you have chosen. Simply say to yourself, "Take me to a memory or give me information about _____ , (whatever situation, behavior, feeling, pain, or problem you have selected)."

If you do not have a specific issue and just want to explore whatever comes up, simply tell your mind: "Take me to a memory or give me whatever information would be best for me now to learn the truth about myself (or that I need for my recovery now)." Ask the question gently a couple of times in your mind and then wait.

Avoid trying to anticipate or think about what might come up. The answer will float up into your mind all by itself, without any conscious effort. Be patient. When you first use the Process, it may take quite a while for a memory to arise. You might focus on your breathing or picture clouds or a flower in your mind so that you are not forcing a response or anticipating what it will be. Allow your subconscious mind to work on its own. Keep your mind free and allow whatever comes up to be there.

The response will come from somewhere deeper than the conscious part of your brain. It may take several moments, especially at first, so be patient and give yourself plenty of time. Just relax and be with the silence; allow the answer to float into your mind by itself, without forcing it.

Until you are familiar with the Process and become comfortable accessing your subconscious, you may not obtain much information. However, the answers and memories you need will come when you are ready, though they may not be at all what you consciously expect. You may get thoughts, mental pictures, sounds, smells, emotions or bodily sensations. Whatever happens is fine. Trust your own process; it will always be right for you.

One note of caution: If you experience terror or feelings that you want to hurt yourself, or if you suspect any type of ritualistic or group abuse, you need the support of a therapist who specializes in dealing with extreme trauma. You can use the Process with your therapist to help you uncover the cause of your emotions and eliminate the effects of any brainwashing. People may have programmed your mind so that you will be afraid of therapy and will not seek help. If you realize that this is a possibility, you need to get help and override the programming. You can override the programming; many cult survivors have. You have ultimate control over your own mind.

Obtain Complete Information

Once something starts to come up, do your best to discover the whole story. Remain aware of your adult mind observing your experience and do your best to obtain as much information about the situation as you can. Picture the situation in your mind with as much detail as possible.

Ask yourself how old you were at the time of the memory. Then find out where you are. Who is with you? Try to picture the details of your surroundings and obtain as much visual and sensory information about the situation as possible. What are you wearing? Are there any smells or sounds? What are your thoughts? What are you feeling in your mind and your body?

Experiment with controlling the way you retrieve memories. If you start to see a little piece of a memory, ask your mind to move forwards or backwards, as though you were running a movie in your mind. Sometimes you can gain more information about an event by backing up and finding out how it started. If a memory is distressing, you can speed it up and proceed through it faster. You will find that you can intensify memories, speed them up, slow them down, or stop them and come out of the state of relaxation. Remind yourself often that whatever you experience is just a memory, just thoughts from the past, even though the situation may feel very real.

Recalling these memories may be frightening, but when you learn that you have control over your memories, you will see that they are just past thoughts that cannot kill you. You have already survived the actual events, and you survived them when you were a child who did not have the maturity and ability you have now to understand. You will survive recovering the memories because you survived the reality.

Releasing Emotions

If you begin to feel strong emotions, remind yourself that the emotions are from the past and that you can handle them now. Allow yourself to feel the emotions fully, express them verbally, and let them flow through you. You have control over your emotions and can stop them whenever you want.

However, the purpose of this process is to let your old feelings out, not to cut them off. Psychologically, what you resist persists. The more you resist a feeling, the stronger it becomes. In order to heal, you need to release the old trapped emotions by feeling them and allowing them to flow through you. When you cut feelings off, they remain inside your mind and body. The more emotion you are able to release the better. If you allow yourself to really feel the emotion, even intensify it, you'll find that you have control over the emotion and it will flow through you and diminish.

When you begin to feel the emotions you felt as a child, do not push them away—simply let them be there and flow through you. If possible, make the feelings more intense. Express your feelings out loud. Scream, cry, curse (God understands that you need to do this to heal), beat your pillows. Talk to the people who hurt you out loud as if they were present. Tell them how you felt about them and what they did to you.

It is best to release as much emotion as possible in each session. However, you do not have to recover all of the old feelings at once; you can always use the Process another time to release more of the emotions in a particular memory.

Unexpressed emotions have physical as well as mental consequences. Tears, for example, have a healing purpose, not just for emotional release, but physical healing. Scientists have found that the chemical composition of tears shed from grief is different from tears shed while peeling an onion. Tears of sorrow release toxins from your body—physical poisons that can cause disease. It is important for your health to cry when you feel sorrow and, if you are unable to cry at the time, to allow the tears to flow as soon as possible. Otherwise the emotions and the toxins they create will remain inside you, poisoning your system.

How to Handle Anger

Our culture frowns on expressions of anger and hatred, but repressing these emotions may also cause stress and disease. All feelings have a purpose: anger is a signal that something is wrong, and hatred can provide the strength to survive painful events. I used to feel guilty about all the anger I found inside me, so I searched through the Bible to find out what it had to say about anger. Surprisingly, it does not say anywhere that anger is wrong. The most specific statement I found was the advice from the Apostle Paul: "Be ye angry, and sin not; let not the sun go down upon your wrath." In other words, don't act on your anger in hurtful ways and don't stuff it. Feel your anger and deal with it as it arises. Don't store it inside you where it will continue to simmer.

Many people vehemently deny that they have any anger inside, but I've never met anyone who doesn't have some suppressed anger. Most people have a deep, subconscious layer of murderous rage accumulated from a variety of large and small hurts they suffered as children. It is this suppressed anger that causes nice, quiet people to kill. When you become aware of this anger and release it in a safe way, it no longer has control over you.

Traditionally, Chinese culture recognizes the importance of accepting anger and hatred without fear or aversion. Chinese parents do not tell their children to "be good" as Americans do, implying that children are not naturally good. Instead the Chinese instruct their children to "embrace the tiger," to embrace the angry, savage thoughts and feelings inside themselves. The Chinese culture accepts the fact that children have to learn to acknowledge and accept their anger so it does not control them.

How to Handle Intense Emotions

If you find your emotions becoming too intense during this process, remind yourself to keep breathing as deeply as possible. This will allow the feelings to flow through you more easily. When you experience trauma, the intense emotions cause you to hold your breath and breathe more shallowly, preventing you from obtaining as much oxygen as you need to dispel the emotional energy. It is this old energy that must be released for total healing to take place. If you breathe deeply and keep your spine straight, arms and legs uncrossed, hands open, the emotional energy will be able to flow freely out of your body.

At times you may begin to feel an emotion before you have any information about the event that caused it. As soon as you recognize the feeling, ask your mind to give you more information about why you are feeling that way. Allow yourself to feel the emotion as intensely as possible, observing the sensations in your mind and body, and ask yourself, "When did I have these feelings before?"

Whenever you use this process, do your best to obtain as many facts about each memory and let out as much emotion as possible so that you don't have to go back to the memory again. Release your feelings for at least fifteen or twenty minutes. It is best to keep expressing your emotions until they are completely exhausted or until you feel a shift take place in your mind or body.

How to Handle Body Memories

Many people experience sensations in various parts of their bodies before they recover visual memories or information about traumatic events. Some people have bodily sensations with their visual memories. These body memories come from the stress and pain the body felt when something traumatic occurred. Since you have neurotransmitters and other brain mechanisms throughout your body, not just in your brain as was previously believed, stress and pain from trauma are recorded in your body as well as in your mind. You need to be release this bodily stress and pain in order for healing to occur.

It is normal to be afraid of encountering these pains or sensations, but you can handle them. They are simply memories of old events, and like mental memories, body memories are muted and less painful than the actual events you have already survived. These sensations do not last and usually are released when the memory of what caused them is recovered.

When you feel a pain or other sensation in your body, use your mind to go inside to explore it and ask your mind to show you a memory or give you information about the cause. If the sensation is uncomfortable, direct your mind to speed up the memories you are recovering and to go through them at whatever speed is best for you.

People are often afraid that if they regain body memories of physical traumas, such as convulsions, passing out, or even temporary death experiences, that the physical conditions will reoccur in the present. This does not happen. These memories and feelings have been trapped in your body for years and you have not physically reexperienced them. You may feel some of the sensations but you will not induce the physical conditions by releasing the memories and feelings. If you reexperience memories of being in a terrible automobile accident where your bones were broken, your bones will not break again when you recall memories of how it felt to be in that accident. The fear you feel now comes from the old fear you felt when the events were actually occurring.

I experienced many body memories. In fact I frequently felt pain before recalling the memory of what caused it. The first time I had a body memory, an unexplained pain in my pelvis, I was terrified because I did not know what was happening and could not make the pain go away. My therapist explained what body memories were and told me they would disappear when I recovered the memory that was causing it. My body sensations persisted until I fully understood what had happened to cause the sensation, recovered the memory, and released the emotions that came with it. Then the body memories disappeared, thankfully forever. Each time I dealt with a body memory, I saw that I could get through it and the next one was easier to face and resolve.

Managing these body sensations taught me a valuable lesson. The first few times I was shaking with fear, not knowing if the sensations would ever stop or if they would become unbearable. Time after time I saw that my fears were always worse than what I actually experienced. I learned that fear always makes experiences more difficult and that where there is fear, there is illusion. Every time I was frightened, I found I had a false belief or needed to obtain more information about the situation. Everything becomes easier when you discover the truth, even about something as painful as sexual abuse, because as soon as you discover the truth you can begin to deal with it. If you are trapped in fear of the unknown, you cannot escape. But knowing the cause of your problems is the key to your prison. When you know the truth, you can deal with it—and heal.

Reassure Yourself

During this process, if you find a painful memory of something that happened when you were a small child, you may want to talk to yourself the way you would talk to a small child. Tell your child self that you will take care of him or her and that you will accept and believe what you discover. If you have a child of your own or know a child the same age as you are in your memory, comfort yourself the way you would comfort that child.

Remind yourself that you are able to take care of yourself now, that you are in control of this situation and can handle these emotions, and that your adult and child selves need to work together to release the old emotions so that you can heal. Continue to reassure yourself frequently that it is safe for you to feel the emotions now, that you have both the intelligence and ability to deal with this situation that you did not have when you were a child. Keep in mind that you have already survived the reality and that now you are just dealing with past thoughts.

Sometimes when I work on a particularly distressing memory, I ask a religious figure to be with me and support me. Other times I pray for help, understanding, and enlightenment. Do whatever you need to make yourself feel safe.

Become an observer of your feelings. Ask your adult self to observe the various sensations the emotions produce in your body and mind. How does your head feel? What about your chest, your shoulders, your stomach, your legs and arms? Describe the sensations to yourself: do you feel a stabbing pain, choking, strangling, burning, coldness, or something else? Label the emotion you are feeling: is it fear, anger, rage, hatred, confusion, grief, or a combination of feelings?

Observe your feelings without judging them. There are no "good" or "bad" feelings; feelings simply are. Emotions are natural and must be respected. Feelings become harmful only when we act on them in harmful ways or when we stuff them and they remain trapped in our bodies.

Change Self-Defeating Beliefs

The next step in the Process, after you have released most of the emotions but while you are still in the relaxed state, is to ask yourself, "What did I decide or conclude about myself based on this experience?" Most people have made negative or limiting decisions about themselves based on pain they have suffered, lies people have told them, and erroneous conclusions about events. These decisions can be changed more effectively and permanently if you analyze them while you are still feeling the old emotions. It is crucial to clear out all of these decisions so that they no longer subconsciously influence your life.

For each traumatic event, you may find several decisions you made about yourself. Some common decisions people make are that they are somehow bad, at fault, worthless, stupid, damaged, flawed, or unlovable. One of the most common myths children believe is that they are not lovable or are somehow defective because no one loved them.

I would tell my clients to picture important people in their minds, look at them closely, and decide if those people were well-adjusted and happy, the kind of people whose opinions are reliable. Usually, visualizing someone who hurt you will reveal the fact that what they did was their problem, not yours. The truth is that if an adult hurts a child or cannot feel love for a child, it is *always* the adult's fault, not the child's.

You may have decided that you had to be perfect, you would not love anyone again, no one cared about you, disaster would always occur, or you did not want to live on this earth. Other decisions may not be as dramatic. You may have decided that you are good at reading and writing, but that you cannot do math. The truth is that, in the absence of certain types of brain damage, anyone can learn any subject. The way you are taught and what you believe about your abilities determine what you can learn.

Criticism when you were feeling vulnerable as a child can limit your ability to learn certain subjects. One woman, a therapist, recovered memories of failing a math exam in high school and feeling devastated because she had been doing well in all of her classes until then. She found that, based on her bewilderment by this unexpected failure, she not only had decided she could not do math but that she could not do anything that involved numbers or "business." As an adult, these decisions prevented her from even writing an effective business letter.

Explore each of your decisions separately and use the adult part of your mind to analyze whether each is a decision that serves you as an adult. If not, use your adult self to convince your child self to change the decision.

In most instances you will discover that when you made the decision you were a child and children often make decisions that seem logical to them but are not logical from an adult perspective. Sometimes your child self may be resistant and you may have to use many arguments and examples to help the child change the decision. Reason with the child in your mind until the child is completely convinced to let go of the old beliefs. No matter how illogical or destructive the belief, remember that at the time of the trauma the belief seemed logical, and its purpose was somehow to protect you. (An exception is when someone else programmed the belief into your mind.)

To help you reevaluate your self-defeating beliefs, ask yourself whether as a child you had all the facts. Did you really understand the situation? Most of us were told a great many lies by the people who hurt us. Some lies were deliberate and others were the result of ignorance. Unfortunately, children are harmed in either case because they believe the adults on whom they depend for their survival.

Picture in your mind the person who hurt you. What did that person tell you? It is important to hear the words the person used because it is the lies you were told then that limit you now.

Using your the adult part of your mind, carefully examine if what the person said was true. Did that person have all of the facts? Do you have all of the facts about the memory? Did that person seem happy and well-adjusted? Who was really to blame? Think of one of your own children or a child you know and put that child in your place. Would that child deserve to be treated as you were? Would you say that child was bad? Would that child have been able to prevent what happened or do it differently?

Continue mentally talking to your adult self and your child selves until you feel a shift inside your mind and body. Talk until you are sure that your child self is convinced of the truth and has accepted a new, more accurate belief. Then go on to the next decision you made and work on that one until you feel a shift. Go through as many decisions about yourself as you can uncover.

Next, ask yourself in your mind, "What did I decide about people—other people in general, men, women, this type of person, and this particular person—based on this situation?" Common conclusions are that people are untrustworthy, dangerous, deceitful, and that they will hurt, abandon, and betray you. You may believe no one will ever care about you, or that you must find ways to please others so that they will not hurt you. Analyze and reevaluate each harmful decision about other people.

When you have finished analyzing decisions about other people, ask yourself what you decided about the universe, life, God, religion, fate, and love based on the situation and use the redecision process again, asking yourself what the initial decision was and whether you want to keep it. Healthy spiritual beliefs inspire people and make them feel good about themselves. You can have healthy spiritual beliefs without following any specific religion or even believing in God, but it is essential to have a positive view of your future, life in general, and your place in the universe. People who have a negative view of life and God, often also have low self-esteem. Perceptions of a universe or deities that are punitive, judgmental, or unforgiving may impede your ability to love yourself and others.

Beliefs about the universe, God, life, and love are usually based on the actions of an authority figure in your childhood, and are often a personification of the worst traits of the people who hurt you the most. Common negative beliefs are that love, life, and the universe are dangerous and capricious, and that God was punishing you or did not care about you. You may need to carefully reexamine all of your spiritual beliefs and explore many religions, as I did, in order to create a personal spiritual philosophy that is supportive and positive. Ask your self whether your beliefs help you by making you feel peaceful and happy, or hurt you by making you feel uncomfortable and scared. In other words, do these beliefs serve you now?

To be sure that you have cleared all destructive decisions about a particular incident, ask yourself if there are any other decisions you need to examine. Take the time to be certain you have cleared out all harmful decisions associated with this incident. Ask yourself if there is anything more you need to know during this session.

Finally, before you stop, ask if there is anything else you need to know or do in order to help your child self heal this memory. Ask what your child self needs and give it: love, to be mentally taken to a safe place, a promise to listen to more at a later time, or whatever else the child asks—within reason of course. As the adult, you are in charge and can negotiate if your child makes unreasonable demands. If you cannot fulfill a request, explain why. You must be honest with your child self in order to encourage trust.

Remember to thank your child self for sharing the memory with you; and thank yourself for doing this process and giving yourself the gift of healing.

What If You Have Difficulty Changing a Belief?

You may encounter some beliefs so strong that your adult mind is unable to convince your child parts to change them. These deep-seated beliefs are usually imprinted by many lies and therefore require more attention. When I could not convince a child part to give up a negative belief, I found that it was usually because I had to recall more facts about the event first. If a belief does not change, you generally need to obtain more information.

However, in a few other instances, even when I thought I had all of the facts, the negative belief was so deep-seated that I still could not convince myself to change it. When that happened, I relied on a technique discovered by psychiatrist Milton Erickson in which I directed my subconscious to change the belief in the best possible way to heal me. Then I would clear my mind and rest in a state of relaxation, without giving my mind any further instructions. After a while, I would feel a shift in my mind and body indicating that the belief had changed. On a few occasions, I did not feel any shift but did not want to stay in the state of relaxation any longer. I instructed my mind to continue to work to change the belief while I was going about my daily activities, and then I came out of the state of relaxation. By the end of the day, I could feel that the belief had shifted.

Some complex clusters of beliefs, such as those about the nature of God/love/the universe, may require more work. Despite several spiritual experiences, I had to do a lot of reading and studying to create a positive cosmic belief system that erased my fears and felt good inside my mind and body. I also had to spend time observing the world with the deliberate intention of looking for kindness and changing my dispiriting beliefs.

Returning to a Positive State of Mind

As a last step in this process, you might want to use a mind-calming technique before you resume your normal activities. One effective technique is to mentally imagine a safe and beautiful place. This technique is described in the nurturing exercise on page 124. Or you may want to repeat a comforting prayer or visualize a loved one, a religious figure, or a happy experience so that you complete this exercise in a positive frame of mind.

After you have used the Process to uncover a number of distressing memories, you might want to use the exercise on page 77 for discovering the original happy, loving child inside of you. Experiment to find what works best to help you return to a calm state of mind.

Summary of the Process

Here is a summary of the main steps of the Inner Exploration Process that you may want to keep available as a reference the first few times you use the Process.

1. Take deep slow breaths and use progressive muscle relaxation and the stair technique to reach a deep state of relaxation.

2. Ask your mind to take you back to a memory or give you information about whatever situation, behavior, feeling, pain, or problem you choose. Or ask your mind to take you back to a memory and give you whatever information you need right now to discover the truth about yourself.

3. Obtain as much information about a memory, feeling, or bodily sensation as possible.
   - How old were you?
   - Where were you?
   - Who was with you?
   - What happened and how did you feel?

4. Feel and release as much emotion as you can.

5. Observe the reactions of your mind and body, reassure yourself, and ask for more information.

6. Uncover and reevaluate all of the unconscious decisions and self-defeating beliefs you made during and as a result of the incident, including beliefs about
   - yourself
   - people in general, men, women, specific people
   - God, fate, life, love and the universe.

Be sure to check for other decisions and for anything else you need to do to resolve the situation and make the child part of you feel cared for and safe.

7. Use a technique to put yourself in a calm state of mind. Focus on something positive.

8. After you have used the Process several times to recover distressing memories, use it to discover your happy, loving child self—the child you were before you were hurt, the child you still are.

3

What Are the Benefits of Clearing Your Past?

The greatest discovery of my generation is that a human being can alter his life by altering his attitudes of mind.

—William James

I asked this question frequently as I struggled on my own healing journey. Many times I became discouraged and overwhelmed by the painful memories and feelings I had uncovered. I wondered whether facing my past was worthwhile. Once, when I was experiencing a great deal of distress, I even paid for a consultation with the director of the psychiatric unit of a prestigious hospital. I wanted to know whether recovering traumatic memories was good for me or whether I should stop. His answer was that if I wanted to heal, the trauma had to come out. He advised me to continue to uncover the trauma I had suppressed.

He also said that, as I released my suppressed emotions, I would reach a point where I could just say "So what?" about my traumatic experiences as a child. "'So what?!'" I screamed at him. "How can I ever say 'So what?' to having been raped, beaten, and tortured by my own father? It's very easy for you to say, but you haven't been through it." He calmly pointed out that my abuse had occurred over thirty years ago and that the memories were coming out because it was time for me to let them go.

I was furious at his callousness, but he turned out to be right. A little over a year later, I told my therapist I was *bored* by the stream of traumatic memories I was still uncovering; even though each was somewhat different, the paralyzing horror and fear were gone. I had released fury, hatred, pain, grief, and fear, and I could truly say "So what?" to the whole business. Although I continued to work on other memories for several years to change my residual patterns and damaging decisions, I could be more analytical when a new unpleasant memory popped up. I even released intense emotions without feeling devastated. Now I can talk about even the most gruesome details without feeling strong emotions. And I cannot begin to describe how much better, lighter, and more peaceful I feel inside.

There are too many dramatic changes in the way I feel to recount them all. The way I see the world and interact with other people is totally different from before. Instead of viewing the world as hostile and dangerous, and people as hurtful and untrustworthy, I see miracles, kindness and caring all around me. No, I'm not a Pollyanna, blind to the world's problems, but when I began to understand myself and treat myself with compassion, I learned to forgive the foibles of others and have compassion for them. After I released what seemed like bottomless anger, I found it easier to understand and forgive the people who hurt me, as well as those who hurt others. I realized that I was not the only one who had suffered immeasurable pain. And I knew that people are controlled by unresolved past experiences and may not be able to make other choices.

I am certainly not the only person who has experienced miracles by using the Inner Exploration Process to clear my past. These techniques have been around for thousands of years, and millions of people have benefitted from them. One of my former clients recently wrote to thank me, saying, "It's strange being in the same place and yet being such a different person." Another woman told me that by releasing her past pain, she had found the "peace that passeth understanding," an inner peace that sustained her even while she was facing the challenges of a bitterly contested divorce. She had an inner certainty that everything would work out for the best. And a man who released the pain and rage at having been sodomized by an uncle said, after seeing himself in my bathroom mirror, that he looked ten years younger. He found it hard to believe the changes in his physical appearance and how much calmer he felt inside simply by releasing old pain.

The changes I have seen in myself and many other people who use the Inner Exploration Process are so numerous it's impossible to describe them all. Obviously, each person's experience is unique. But in general, clearing the past increases self-esteem, improves relationships, and enables people to find greater inner peace and happiness.

Perhaps the most life-altering benefit of clearing your past is that you'll be able to change the dozens of subconscious negative decisions and beliefs about yourself. Studies show that approximately 70 percent of the population has low self-esteem. Since most of us have suffered some hurt, rejection, abandonment, or other painful events, we are troubled by worries, fears, doubts, and intrusive thoughts that prevent us from loving ourselves. Our experiences do not have to be as dramatic as physical or sexual abuse; emotional abuse and feelings of being unloved can also affect our self-esteem. We all have been hurt and invalidated and have believed lies about ourselves. A collection of small hurts and lies can be as damaging as large ones. It's amazing how events that may seem insignificant when we think about them consciously as adults can have such a profound effect on a child's mind, producing such deep, and often negative, feelings that cause personality changes.

Karen's experience is an example of how a seemingly innocuous comment can have long-lasting effects. For much of her life, Karen believed she was flighty, an "airhead," and her behavior seemed to support this description. When she was in her twenties, Karen began to explore her mind to find out why she acted irresponsibly and forgot things. She remembered an incident as a teenager when she had just started driving and she and her mother were discussing buying her a car. Her mother said that Karen should get a car with an automatic gearshift because, she said, "You can be kind of an airhead at times, and I don't think you're responsible enough to drive a stick shift." This casual comment stuck with Karen and she realized that she had internalized her mother's description of her personality and used it to justify acting irresponsibly and making mistakes.

After further mental examination, Karen remembered earlier trauma that also contributed to her limiting beliefs. Karen's parents divorced when she was eight years old and she was shuttled back and forth between her father and mother weekly for over a year. The distress of the divorce and constantly switching homes were traumatic to Karen and made her forgetful; she would often lose things during the weekly changes of location. Her parents' annoyance at Karen's forgetfulness caused further trauma and began the pattern that continued to haunt Karen as an adult. Uncovering this childhood trauma helped Karen change her beliefs about her ability to act responsibly, and her flighty behavior changed. She is now an executive at a growing company, where she ably handles many responsibilities and details. As this examples demonstrates, if you clear out this old baggage, you have more options, more choices of how to think, feel, and react, instead of thinking, feeling, and reacting the same way you did when something painful occurred in your childhood.

Another major benefit is the effect clearing our past has on relationships. We tend to treat others the way we were treated as children. It is a perverse fact that we often incorporate the negative behaviors of the people who hurt us the most, subconsciously believing that somehow imitating our abusers will give us their power. I was horrified to find that I had picked up my father's sarcasm and arrogance, as well as a cold, piercing way he had of looking at people when he felt threatened. Even if you are consciously aware of such behaviors, it is difficult to change them without clearing out the trauma that caused them. But when you release the emotions and uncover the destructive decisions you made, the behaviors usually vanish without any further effort.

Uncovering past trauma can also eliminate destructive patterns that seem to repeat themselves in intimate relationships. If you seem to repeatedly be attracted to partners who betray or abandon you, you may be trapped in one of these patterns. A woman whom I will call Rayne had been given up for adoption at the age of six weeks because her sixteen-year-old, unwed mother had no money to care for her. Rayne had always felt worthless and unlovable because she believed her mother had not wanted her. Her beliefs made relationships difficult because her fear of abandonment caused her to push people away. She was considering divorce at the time she consulted me.

Rayne unconsciously believed that since she was worthless, anyone who loved her had to be worthless, too. She also followed a common pattern where people push loved ones away so the loved one won't abandon them unexpectedly. As destructive as this pattern is, it persists because it gives people a feeling of control over their fate. Using the Inner Exploration Process, Rayne was able to recover a memory of being held by her mother who smiled down at her and sang to her. Rayne felt her mother's love. The realization that her mother had loved her eradicated many negative conclusions Rayne had drawn about being unloved and unlovable. Once she felt worthy of being loved, she stopped pushing away love, and her relationship with her husband and children dramatically improved.

I have seen many relationships improve dramatically after people clear out old wounds and mistaken beliefs. Clearing the parts of my mind that contained beliefs I held that I could never depend on anyone allowed me to become closer to people, develop better relationships, and have more caring friends. After eliminating old patterns based on distrust and worthlessness, I became less defensive and better able to accept criticism. I came to know that, no matter what others may think, I am a good person and I deserve to be treated well. Instead of always taking care of other people, I now also take care of myself. I no longer try to please people who hurt me or tolerate their destructive actions. Ironically, in my role as a lawyer I was successful in protecting the rights of others, but it took me over fifty years to eradicate deep-seated patterns of victimization and helplessness and to learn to stand up for myself. My life is so much easier now. I don't have to try so hard all the time.

Many people are caught in patterns where they are repeatedly victimized as adults; they become involved in situations where others frequently betray, lie, cheat, or abuse them. These patterns of revictimization are almost always based on childhood trauma, especially where people marry abusers or are raped several times. I want to stress that these people do not consciously choose or cause these acts to occur; they do not "ask for it." But because of the suppressed pain inside them, they unconsciously act like victims and attract abusers. Uncovering the repressed causes of these patterns makes them disappear. Men and women who used to be attracted to abusive partners can avoid abusers and choose a different kind of partner.

People who are trapped in destructive patterns where they hurt others can also be helped by clearing their pasts. When they release old rage and pain, rage-aholics find that their extreme anger is no longer triggered by minor events, and they are able to perceive most events as minor. Parents who uncover the pain they suffered as children when hit by their parents no longer strike their own children. But the healings I have seen of child molesters are the most dramatic examples of the way clearing the past can change victimizer behavior. Jimmy, a former client and now a friend, was brutally physically and sexually abused by his mother and her boyfriends. Because of the abuse, the court took Jimmy away from his mother when he was seven and placed him with his father, in spite of a psychological report and other evidence that the father was also abusive. Jimmy was sodomized by his father until his father died when Jimmy was fourteen. Jimmy was then placed in various foster homes where he continued to be abused.

A couple of years later, complaints began to be filed with the police that Jimmy was molesting younger children, but Jimmy vigorously denied the allegations. He had no memory of the incidents. Jimmy's mind had also blocked out the years of sodomy and other abuse by his father; in fact, by that time Jimmy had idealized his father, claiming that his father had loved him and taken good care of him. This idealization of an abuser by an abused child is common. Therapists used various behavioral techniques without success to try to make Jimmy confess to molesting other children and to change his victimizing behavior. It was not until another therapist used the Inner Exploration Process to help Jimmy remember his father's abuse and release the pain, rage, and helplessness he had felt as a child that Jimmy was able to recall his molestation of younger children. Jimmy was horrified and grief-stricken to learn what he did to other children and he is working hard to heal himself, help others, and make amends. He no longer is tempted to molest children. His life and behavior have totally changed. In his words, "I have gotten off the roller coaster and I have found people who are nice to me. I know I am here for a purpose and I am going find a way to help other people like me."

I have seen many cases where child molesters have used the Inner Exploration Process to uncover their own childhood sexual abuse and heal. A teenage girl I will call Jewel was able to use the Process to release her pain and rage at her father who molested her, while her father was also uncovering his memories and feelings in therapy. Jewel, who used to be very angry and did not do well in school, now makes straight As and is applying to college. After her father completed his therapy and begged her forgiveness, Jewel was able to forgive him and they are now good friends. These examples are not unique; many people who used to victimize others have been able to heal once they uncovered and healed their own pain and took responsibility for their actions.

Most people have no idea what it is like to really feel peaceful and content. They are numb, going through their daily routines like robots, never experiencing real joy or peace. Much of the time, people are unaware of their constant anxiety and inner stress; they think what they feel is normal, that everyone must feel the same way, because they don't talk about how they feel inside and therefore have no means of comparison. In fact, I had never realized how terrible I felt until Anne, a woman sexually abused as a child for eight years by her brother, said that she had felt all of her life as though wolves were tearing her apart inside. She thought her feelings were normal until she dealt with the memories and anguish she had felt as child, and her inner pain disappeared. She told me she felt a peace she had not known was possible.

As she described her transformation, I suddenly realized I had felt the same pain inside for most of my life, but that after clearing my past I no longer felt that way. Each time I uncovered more memories and changed my limiting beliefs, little by little—in a process so gradual that at first I did not notice the changes—my inner turmoil, tension, and terror somehow metamorphosed into tranquility. Afterwards, it was difficult for me to imagine how I had survived the inner agony I had lived with and ignored for so many years.

Exploring your mind can reveal the causes of so many unexplained problems: insomnia, stress, depression, fear, physical discomfort, strange reactions, and so on. It is so liberating to know that there are reasons for the ways you act and feel, and that you aren't crazy or deliberately doing strange or harmful things. Uncovering my own painful childhood events was a blessing for me because I found that all of my bizarre thoughts, nightmares, and behaviors had a logical basis. Many of my clients expressed the same relief after recovering long-forgotten events and discovering that what they thought were immutable personality defects were simply mistaken beliefs. Freedom comes from understanding the root of your problems, because once you find the root you can pull it out and plant something new.

Clearing Your Past Can Accelerate Spiritual Growth

Most people have had mystical or spiritual experiences; in fact, a Gallup poll indicates that over 70 percent of the population has had at least one such experience. Using the Inner Exploration Process often increases the number of such experiences because it helps people uncover their true selves—their spirits. Psychological problems limit spiritual progress; the old baggage weighs you down. If you've been trapped in a prison of fear and self-hatred, you may be oblivious to serendipity and the "coincidences," kindness and love that enfold you. I saw only cruelty, betrayal, and violence, because that is what I had been programmed to see. My mother used to quote the poet John Milton: "The mind is its own place and in itself can make a hell of heaven, a heaven of hell." Changing my mental program literally changed my world from hell to heaven.

As you become clearer, you become more in touch with your true nature because you eliminate the barrier of fear that creates the illusion that you are separate from God, truth, love, the universe, and other people. It took several years to erase all of the lies I believed about myself, and to change self-hatred to love. But when I took the time to clear my past, I found a new me and unlimited freedom.

People who use the Inner Exploration Process sometimes retrieve memories from their childhoods in which beings of bright light consoled them during particularly difficult periods, such as during severe illness or abuse. When they recover these intense feelings of having been loved, even though their physical pain may have continued, these people are often transformed by the experience. In some cases, people who use the Inner Exploration Process report retrieving early memories of God or where they were before this life, and these memories produce spiritual as well as psychological healing.

Many people gain spiritual knowledge when they use the Inner Exploration Process to discover their true selves—who they were before they were hurt and believed the lies they were told. Several cases are described in the chapter 6. Using the Process to retrieve memories of myself before I was abused showed me beyond any doubt that, as an infant, I had been an innocent, loving little being who only wanted to love and be loved. I was also blessed with a vision that, despite appearances, there is a Plan and everything will turn out all right.

However, even with all of the changes in myself, I still have problems and am still learning and growing. I feel infinitely better and believe I am a nicer person because I cleared away my old baggage, but I do not have wings or a halo. Despite my spiritual experiences, at times I fall back into the illusion of the external world and despair, but those times no longer last for weeks. Now I can nurture myself and pull myself out of the doldrums, or find someone who can help me. When I feel upset, I now realize that what I am feeling is probably coming from something still unresolved in my past and I can uncover the cause and move on. I know healing is a process not a destination; we continue to grow and learn throughout our lives.

Anyone can reach this state of clarity and peace. I have met people who were former inmates of concentration camps, self-confessed murderers, molesters, and others who have suffered unspeakable horrors, all of whom transformed and healed. There is no one, no matter what was done to them or what they have done, who cannot heal. Everyone can heal. I want to repeat this because so many people have been brainwashed and told lies to the contrary.

The truth is that you can heal, no matter what was done to you or what you have done. There are no exceptions.

Would I go through the stress of recovering memories again in order to get to where I am today? Yes! Without a moment's hesitation. I believe clearing my past was more than worth the effort. Even though the process may sometimes seem endless and you may feel that you are not making any progress, I promise you that one day you will wake up and feel so differently about your life and yourself you will be grateful for the incredible gift of healing you have given yourself.

Unleash Your Potential and Creativity

Some people fear that if they clear out past trauma, their basic personalities will be altered and they somehow will cease to exist. Actually the opposite is true. By clearing your past, you become more you—the person you were meant to be before your potential was limited by pain and lies. You find your true self when you peel away the layers of defenses, falsehood, and fear—the misconceptions that conceal your soul.

When you become aware of what you are doing, feeling, and thinking, you have more choices. You can choose the characteristics and beliefs you want to keep and those you want to change or eliminate. You will not lose any trait or talent or part of yourself you want to keep; you will only lose the fear, anger, and pain that are limiting your options and restricting your ability to feel joy and love.

The myth that neurosis and suffering are requisites to creativity is perpetuated by people who are afraid to face their problems. I grew up around neurotic movie stars, writers, and directors in Hollywood who were convinced that whatever they gained in mental health, they would lose in creativity. They wore their neuroses like a badge. Bizarre and even destructive behavior was not only excused but encouraged—anything was tolerated for the sake of "art." But you do not have to cut off an ear to be a great painter. Neurotic artists succeed in spite of their neuroses, not because of them. Unhappiness does not create talent; it impedes and destroys it, as many famous people who have self-destructed illustrate. Suffering does not make anyone more talented; suffering makes it harder to work productively. The main symptoms of depression are loss of interest and pleasure in activities formerly enjoyed, fatigue, and the inability to think and concentrate—conditions hardly conducive to brilliant creative expression.

I witnessed a dramatic example of how childhood events can affect creativity when a writer friend of mine, whom I will call Ray, sought my help. He was writing a children's book and, although his ideas had been coming easily and he was pleased with the story, he had not been able to write for a couple of months. He was distressed and wanted to know how to get over his "writer's block" so he could finish his book.

Ray said he had tried all sorts of techniques to get over the block but that nothing had worked. I suggested using the Inner Exploration Process as a way to reach the heart of the problem quickly. Ray was skeptical and said he had difficulty relaxing and did not think he could reach subconscious memories, but he agreed to try. After we used progressive muscle relaxation and he visualized walking down stairs, his body relaxed.

Then I asked his mind, his total intelligence that knew everything about him, to take him back to a memory that would explain why he had writer's block and could not finish his book. Ray rapidly went from a state of relaxation to one of terror, and came abruptly out of the relaxed state. He said he was experiencing the same chaotic emotions he felt when he tried to meditate; he believed he was feeling "the chaos of the universe" and could not continue with the Process. I told Ray that he was not experiencing cosmic chaos but strong emotions he had stored in his mind and body from past trauma. Ray had a difficult time accepting the fact that what he was feeling was caused by something traumatic he had experienced as a child, but he agreed to return to a state of relaxation.

I asked Ray's mind to show him a memory that would explain his chaotic feelings. His breathing became very rapid and he recovered a vivid memory of his father beating him with a belt. When I asked how old he was, he said, "Four." Ray felt overwhelming terror, pain, betrayal, grief, shame, anger, hatred, guilt and confusion—the chaotic emotions the beating engendered in him as a child. He was so young when he was beaten that his father and mother comprised his universe, and being beaten therefore created universal chaos for him.

After he released his painful emotions, I asked Ray what thoughts he had when he was being beaten. He said he thought that he must have done something wrong and be really bad because his father was punishing him so severely. He also concluded that his father must not love him because his father was hurting him so much; and, since Ray did not understand what he had done to deserve the beating, he assumed he was not lovable.

After Ray spent almost an hour examining and changing his childhood misconceptions, he used the Process to ask his mind if there was anything else he needed to know that would explain his writer's block. Ray quickly recalled his father repeatedly saying he wanted to be proud of Ray. As a child, Ray hated his father so much because of the beatings that Ray swore he would never do anything to make his father proud of him. Although his conscious mind had long forgotten that childhood vow, Ray had unconsciously acted on it for more than thirty years. Ray's repressed hatred for his father and his childhood vow were responsible not only for Ray's writer's block, but for his failure to allow himself to achieve any kind of professional success in his life. Once Ray was able to examine these destructive beliefs, he saw that he no longer needed to punish his father and that he could chose to be successful for himself. Two months later, he sent me the completed manuscript of his book.

As Ray's story illustrates, removing the effects of trauma increases creativity. Unresolved trauma inhibits creativity because repressed memories and emotions are usually stored in the right side of your brain, the side that controls your feelings, creativity, imagination, and intuition. Repressing memories and emotions requires an enormous amount of mental energy and brain capacity. When a large amount of your brain power is devoted to keeping traumatic events out of your consciousness, you simply run out of space for creative functions, the way a computer disk runs out of space when it is filled with information. I was an uptight, left-brained attorney until I began recovering memories, and only then did I even consider writing a book. I did not lose my ability to be logical and rational or practice law; I simply added creativity and intuition to my skills and expanded into a career of writing and lecturing that I enjoy immeasurably more.

Repressed memories also take up space in your brain normally used for short-term memory. When old memories are deleted, short-term memory improves. Releasing suppressed memories will improve your ability to concentrate and you will be able to accomplish more work in shorter periods of time because you will think more clearly.

Fear and suffering contract our minds; clearing our minds expands them. As people release and resolve repressed memories, they become *more* creative because they open up more capacity for creativity in their brains. Clearing out limiting fears opens the way to hearing our inner guidance, our intuition, the still small voice within. We begin to access the vast knowledge of the collective consciousness and creative ideas begin to flow freely.

4

Answers to Questions You May Have about the Process

In the midst of winter I finally discovered within me an invincible summer.

—Albert Camus

When to Seek Professional Help

Using this process may uncover frightening events and emotions, and situations may arise where you may need the help of a professional. If you have thoughts about hurting yourself or others, it is important to realize that those thoughts are based on false beliefs. You should consult a therapist immediately so that you do not become confused and act on your thoughts. Such feelings are not uncommon and are usually caused by past events even though they seem to be based on present circumstances. People who are depressed and feel hopeless usually think they are crazy and incurable. This is not the case. There is a logical reason for your feelings, and you can be healed. No matter how terrible your life appears to be, most of your overwhelming feelings of depression and hopelessness are not coming from present events, but from the feelings you had when something traumatic happened to you as a child.

Children who feel unloved or are being abused have nowhere to turn, feel totally hopeless, and often decide that the only way out is to die. Their feelings of despair, anger, and frustration are so painful that their minds create a part to contain these feelings and block them from the child's consciousness. As adults, if these old emotions are triggered, these people may be overwhelmed by feelings of depression and believe they want to die. If you begin to feel this way, you need to consult a therapist who specializes in treating severe childhood trauma.

You can continue to use the Inner Exploration Process with a therapist to find out why you want to die. It is also important to keep reminding yourself that these are old feelings and that you can survive—you already have. Experiencing the old feelings and knowing *why* you felt that way will neutralize your present feelings of despair. Use your adult mind to convince your hurt part that you are safe now and can learn to be happy. You have already survived the worst. It would be a terrible waste to die now.

The fact that your old suicidal feelings are resurfacing is a signal that you are ready to deal with memories you have suppressed. Your mind is letting you know that you can handle these memories now. Work with a therapist to uncover the memories and release the emotions. Once you bring the memories and emotions of your wounded part to conscious awareness, you will find that your desire to die will disappear.

Sometimes people hear voices when they are alone. Although it may seem as though the voices are coming from outside, the truth is that these voices come from inside the mind. Just as people can have visual flashbacks (waking visions of past traumatic events), they can also have auditory flashbacks. People who have been severely hurt as children can become delusional and think that God wants them to hurt or kill themselves or other people. *If a voice tells you to hurt yourself or another person in any way, it is not coming from God and you need to get professional help immediately.* These voices are coming from wounded parts of your own mind that need to be healed. If you feel like hurting yourself or someone else, call a therapist for help right away. If you don't know one, knock on a neighbor's door or call a friend, but get someone to help you.

Many people have suffered severe trauma as children, such as physical and sexual abuse, and have totally blocked these events from their conscious minds. Statistics show that one-quarter to one-third of the adult population in the United States has been sexually abused before the age of eighteen. If physical abuse and neglect are added to that figure, abused children constitute almost one-half to three-quarters of the population. Similar statistics are coming out of Canada, England, Australia, and

France, where one of every five trials in the Cours d'Assises involves incest. Often people who have been abused as children may consciously believe that their childhoods were happy. Discovering the truth about repressed events can therefore be a tremendous shock and evoke intense emotions.

If you uncover abuse in your childhood, you need to decide whether you can—or want to—handle such discoveries on your own. I recommend that, at least initially, you seek the support of a therapist who specializes in such cases.

Exploring hidden parts of your mind requires uncovering strong emotions, and you may start feeling these emotions even at times when you are not using the Inner Exploration Process. Remind yourself periodically that what you are feeling is old emotion from past events, even though it may seem very real now. It is sometimes helpful to post notes around your home reminding yourself that what you are feeling is coming from memories of events that are over. You might write: "What I am feeling is coming from the past. I need to explore what is responsible for these feelings. If I feel really depressed, I will call _____ (list a few people and a therapist who will be available to support you)."

Although it is important to feel the painful emotions you suppressed so you can release them, it is not healthy to feel them all the time. There is a difference between releasing emotions and wallowing in them. People need a healthy balance in their lives, spending most of their time living in the present moment and enjoying life. If you become stuck in an emotional state and cannot work or perform your normal activities, you should seek professional help.

You need to trust your instincts, and decide when it is best to proceed on your own and when to seek professional help. Working with a facilitator or joining a support group can also be beneficial. An important part of healing is learning to ask for help.

How Long Will This Process Take?

How long this process takes depends on the memories you uncover and how much emotion you feel comfortable dealing with at one time. Generally an hour or two is enough for one session, although sometimes completely recovering and analyzing a memory may take longer.

Don't expect too much of yourself the first couple of times you use the Process. It is a bit of a shock to find memories and emotions emerging from your mind that you had no idea were there. Give yourself time to become familiar with the Process and to learn what works best for you.

When you first begin to use the Process, you may feel safer limiting your sessions to shorter periods until you become familiar with the effects and how your mind works. Later you may choose to spend more time on particular issues. The first few times you use the Process, you may find that it takes quite a while to get in touch with your subconscious. After you use the Process several times, accessing memories will take less time.

If you discover a very traumatic situation, one of which you were not consciously aware, your mind may deal with those memories in small pieces. You may need several sessions to uncover complete information about the event. People's experiences are different, but your mind will always protect you and give you only what you can handle.

Do not force yourself beyond what you feel comfortable dealing with in any one session. If you have thoughts, feelings, or a sense that you need to stop, trust your feelings. As you experiment with the Process, it will become easier and you will be able to handle more. Pushing too hard is not a good idea because you are not treating yourself with respect. You need to honor your limits and work at your own pace, without comparing your progress to that of anyone else. My experience, personally and with clients, is that you will not recover anything you're not ready to resolve, no matter how hard you push. Remember, whatever you experience is right for you.

I learned the hard way that it is imperative to keep a healthy balance between recovering memories and enjoying the present. When I first learned how to use this process, I wanted to recover as many memories as I could and get rid of my pain as quickly as possible. Although I was seeing a therapist once a week, I also used the Process to recover more memories of childhood abuse for several hours every day. I pushed myself too hard and spent too much time reexperiencing past abuse and not enought time nuturing and taking care of myself. I became overwhelmed by too many memories and did not give myself time to assimilate them consciously. I ended up in the psychiatric ward of a hospital, forcing me to rest my mind and deal with what I had uncovered.

Although it is important to always be gentle with yourself, keep in mind that you repressed memories of events as a child because they were frightening and overwhelming at the time. The hurt child in you still thinks that recalling the event will be overwhelming. While some events will certainly be unpleasant to recall, your mind will not allow you to recall them unless you are ready. Your mind has protected you for all of these years and will not let you down now. Reassure your child self that you can handle knowledge of the event now. Proceed when your child self feels safe or agrees to go ahead. Listen to your own mind and decide what is right for you. You control how you use this process.

When you start recovering memories, you may find that you also begin to feel more emotions than you are used to feeling. People often think they are getting worse because they experience feelings of sadness, fear, or anger that they may not be able to control. These reactions are normal and mean that you are healing. You need to release old emotions you have repressed and become familiar with feelings you have denied. Don't resist these feelings; just allow them to be there and know that you will survive them. You may go through uncomfortable periods, but you will find that as you continue to use the Process to obtain more information about the origins of your feelings, their intensity will diminish and you will begin to feel better. Most people have a lot of supressed pain inside them, so be patient with yourself.

People frequently ask me how long they will need to use the Process. I asked this question of my own therapists many times. I wanted to be *done,* like a bun in the oven. But the answer to the question is that there is no answer. I can't give you a number or even an estimate because the time it takes to clear the past is different for every person. Clearing your mind is an ongoing process, not a destination. You may deal with some issues and stop using the Process for a while until a situation arises in your life where you feel a need to use the Process again. I can only tell you that the more limiting beliefs you clear out, the happier you will be.

You can use the Process whenever you choose to throughout your life. The more you practice it, the more familiar you will become with the way your mind works, and your fears and resistance will decrease. You will be able to relax more deeply and recover memories more easily. Each time you face your fears, you will find it easier to deal with other traumatic situations.

In using this process, there is no "right" or "wrong." These are only guidelines for you to use to explore your mind. You may change any part of the Process you choose and tailor it to meet your own needs.

Even after my stay in the hospital, I must confess I continued to use this process almost daily for several years; but I spent less time doing the process each day and took better care of myself—exercising, working, and getting out of the house with friends. I probably spent more time clearing my past than might be necessary for most people, but I had a lot to clear out. Once I realized how enormously my life was dominated by the past, I wanted to be absolutely clear of old patterns. I did not want to be manipulated by past events in any situation. I still use the Process whenever a situation arises where I feel I am reacting too emotionally, feel discomfort in my body, or have difficulty resolving a problem. But now I can get into a relaxed state in a couple of minutes and go through the entire Process in fifteen or twenty minutes—although some issues may take more time. The benefits of clearing my past have been more than worth the time and effort.

What If Nothing Happens?

There are a number of reasons why you may not be able to immediately access memories using the Inner Exploration Process. You may not be sufficiently relaxed and may need to learn how to calm your mind. The simple meditation technique on page 150 and the progressive relaxation technique on page 149 will help you develop the habit of relaxing and quieting your thoughts.

Another possibility is that you may not be ready to work on clearing your past. You may need to use other exercises in this book first to increase your self-esteem, understand yourself, and make yourself physically and emotionally stronger. For example, you many want to use the nurturing exercises in chapter 10 to make the child inside you feel safe and loved before using the Process. Sometimes people hate the child in them because they feel the child was weak and vulnerable. They are afraid of feeling helpless again and therefore reject the child part of them. You must get to know your child self and learn to love that child. Your child must trust you as an adult in order to release suppressed memories and emotions.

You may have stresses in your life that require attention before you can successfully explore past events. If you are under severe stress, exhausted, or ill, you need all your energy to deal with your present circumstances, rather than working on the past. A client of mine, Laura, came to therapy with some conscious memories of having been sexually abused as a child, but believed there was more that she had repressed. She walked into my office carrying her six-week-old baby, pushing a stroller with her one-and-a-half-year-old child, and making sure her three-year-old twins were close by. Her husband was going to school and working full time, and she did not think "good mothers" hired baby-sitters. Laura was totally exhausted.

I told Laura that I did not think she was in any condition to start dealing with past issues because she needed to rest first, but she insisted on trying to recover memories immediately. In spite of her professed readiness and her conscious desire to know more and heal quickly, she was not able to recover any memories. Her subconscious mind knew she was too tired to deal with traumatic memories and protected her in spite of her conscious desires. We worked out a schedule where Laura would have time by herself one afternoon a week and go out alone with her husband one evening a week. After about four weeks, when she was more rested, Laura was able to recover some of her suppressed memories.

Take Care of Yourself

In order to access your subconscious, you must feel safe, relaxed, and comfortable. If you are under pressure at work or at home, it is often best to deal with those issues first, before tackling past events. For example, people in abusive marriages frequently have also been abused as children but find it difficult to work on their childhood abuse until they free themselves from their abusive partner and are in a living situation where they feel safe.

While you naturally want to heal as quickly as possible, it is important to maintain a balance and not push yourself too much. Your mind can process only so much information at a time and, especially if you are dealing with painful events, you may need to rest periodically to absorb what you have discovered. Trust your instincts and do not go faster than feels safe for you. Remember that people heal at different rates. In order to heal you must take good care of yourself and trusting your own process.

Exercise and Meditation

You should always take good care of yourself, but especially when you are uncovering blocked memories. I recommend that you start a program of regular exercise and meditation before beginning to use the Inner Exploration Process. Dealing with past trauma is stressful, and regular exercise is the best way to reduce stress as well as depression. Suggestions about exercise can be found on page 101.

An important part of healing is learning to quiet the thoughts and worries that race around in your mind. People have been plagued with obsessive thoughts probably since the time that homo sapiens developed. Animals do not seem to worry; they deal with what is happening in the present moment. But when we humans became self-aware, we started to worry about ourselves and began to focus more on the past and the future than on the present.

While you are dealing with past trauma, it is essential to know how to turn off thoughts and emotions when necessary. You must have space to focus on tasks you have to do, enjoy activities, and notice the beauty around you. There are many types of meditation that can help you quiet your mind and return to a calm state, and you may want to try those on pages 150 and 169 to find what works best for you. If you practice meditation daily, you will find it transforming.

Join or Form a Support Group

There are free support groups for almost every kind of problem, and it can be helpful to share what you discover through this process with people who have had similar experiences. Consider joining a group that is exploring issues similar to yours. Knowing you can count on people to provide support when you need it can provide the sense of security you need to more easily retrieve disturbing memories.

Try Using the Process with a Facilitator

Only you can clear your mind; no one can do it for you. However, you do not have to always be alone when you do it. It is often helpful to have someone available to support you while you use the Inner Exploration Process. Having someone you trust with you as you go through the Process, particularly the first few times you use it, can be comforting and help you feel safe so you can more easily access subconscious memories. If you feel uncomfortable having someone in the room while you go through the steps of the Process, you may want to arrange for a friend to be available in another room or by phone so you know you have someone to support you.

These days, many people cannot afford to go to a therapist and that is why self-help methods such as the Inner Exploration Process are so important. For centuries people have looked inside themselves, cleared their minds, and discovered their true nature on their own. Most of these people must have struggled to discover for themselves the techniques that are readily available to us today in books, but they succeeded all the same.

Although the Inner Exploration Process can be used with a therapist, one of its advantages is that it can also be used with anyone who volunteers to act as a facilitator. Usually people have a reciprocal relationship with their facilitators and switch roles. The facilitator does not need any special training, only a knowledge of the Process and its purposes, which can be obtained simply by reading your copy of this book. The main purpose of having someone present is to provide support and help you feel safe so that you can do your work more effectively. A facilitator can also help you through the steps of the Process, reassure you, talk you into a deeper state of relaxation, and encourage you to keep recovering memories and fully release emotions.

It is important to select a facilitator you really trust, not someone you think you "should" pick. Both your adult and child selves need to feel safe with the facilitator. Often it is preferable to choose a facilitator who is not a partner or family member because people who are too close to you may become too emotionally involved and try to fix you, instead of allowing you to heal yourself. People who care about you may find it painful to see you in distress and may try to stop you from feeling the emotions you need to release. If loved ones want to be facilitators, they must accept one basic truth: *They cannot fix you.* They are not responsible for your healing; you are.

The Facilitator's Role

Adult Children of Alcoholics have a motto that applies to anyone who volunteers to act as a facilitator: "You didn't cause it and you can't cure it." The facilitator should not try to be a therapist. The best thing a facilitator can do is *listen* and provide unconditional love and support.

The most difficult task for a facilitator is remaining calm while the person using the Process is experiencing strong emotions. These emotions can sometimes seem frightening, and the facilitator may be tempted to cut them off. However, the facilitator must understand that cutting off emotions causes harm. Whatever people feel is what they need to feel and they will survive releasing the feelings. The facilitator needs to be patient and allow feelings to come out for as long as it takes, which in some cases may be several hours. When my grief came out about not having parents who could love me the way I needed to be loved, I cried for five hours. I felt incredibly better afterward, and it would have been a terrible mistake for anyone to have cut off my expression of grief.

A facilitator should always validate the processor's feelings. Most people have had their feelings invalidated, criticized, or ridiculed at some point. You may have been told, "Big kids don't cry," "It's wrong to hate anyone," "Don't let anyone know what you feel," "Put on a happy face," "You shouldn't be angry at someone who has died," and other nonsense. One of the most valuable gifts a facilitator can give is to validate whatever feelings arise. People in distress want to know that what they are feeling is okay—that they are entitled to feel what they feel. Sometimes your feelings may seem unreasonable to others, but that's how you feel. There are no *shoulds* or *shouldn'ts;* feelings simply are.

The facilitator also needs to be honest about his or her own feelings. If something was terrible, say so: "That was really terrible." "That must have been horrible for you." "How awful!" Put the blame where it belongs—on whoever hurt the person: "What a dreadful thing to do to you." "She hurt you so much." Express how sorry you are about what the processor experiences: "I'm sorry your head hurts," or "I'm so sorry you were all alone," or "I'm sorry you didn't get the love you needed and deserved."

The facilitator should take every opportunity to point out how strong the person using the process is. "It's amazing that you survived. How strong you must have been to live through that." Never lie. Everyone has been told enough lies, that's why they need to use the Process. The fact is that the person has survived and had to be very strong to do so. The facilitator should reassure the processor that he or she is safe now—these are just memories. By affirming the processor's strengths and ability to heal, the facilitator helps the truth emerge instead of reinforcing false images of helplessness and worthlessness.

However, during the process, a facilitator should remain silent most of the time to avoid disturbing the processor's state of relaxation. If the processor is stuck or needs reassurance, the facilitator can assist, but should speak in a soft, gentle voice. The facilitator may help deepen the state of relaxation by talking the processor through the progressive relaxation exercise or by reminding him or her to mentally walk down stairs and go "deeper and deeper into relaxation." The facilitator should encourage the processor to keep asking his or her mind for the truth, and to hear the sounds, see the sights, smell the smells, taste the tastes, and feel the feelings the processor needs to recover.

If the processor begins to feel an emotion or body sensation but cannot get any other information, the facilitator should provide reassurance by reminding the processor that whatever he or she experiences is fine and that it's safe to go deeper into the emotion or sensation. The facilitator might ask if there is a child part that needs to be heard or reassured. Sometimes people in distress want the facilitator to hold their hand; others do not want to be touched. You and your facilitator should discuss in advance exactly what the facilitator's role is to be and how much help you want.

There are lots of *don'ts* for facilitators. The most important one is don't judge what the processor experiences. The processor is exploring his or her own mind and whatever comes out needs to come to consciousness. Sometimes what people have experienced may seem bizarre, but if it is in their minds, it is usually true—especially if accompanied by strong emotions or body sensations. When people use the Process, they need to obtain all of the facts about their memories and make their own decisions about how they want to resolve what they recover. They have to decide how they want to deal with what is in their minds, free from outside judgement.

Sometimes processors recover surprising memories of spiritual experiences or have such experiences while using the Process. If the experience is positive, the facilitator should not interrupt or question it.

Instead, the facilitator should encourage the processor to obtain the benefit of the experience (even if the facilitator finds it hard to believe). If the experience is frightening, then the processor really needs help. The facilitator must push aside whatever fear he or she may feel and help the processor find out more about the situation by asking questions that will elicit more information. Often it helps to reassure the processor that he or she is not bad and that God loves him or her no matter what.

Whatever "demons"—fearful or angry parts—that may emerge, there is a logical explanation for them. "Demons" often represent wounded parts of the person's mind or may mask actual people who were hurtful, when the processor is not yet ready to see the truth. In some cases, destructive parts may have been programmed by cult members or others, and may need to be healed by a specialist. If the facilitator feels unable to deal with the situation, he or she should encourage the processor to find professional help.

The facilitator should not give advice or offer solutions. The Process is designed to empower people by helping them discover what is in their minds so that they can make their own choices and decisions. Telling someone what to do only reinforces the recipient's feelings of incompetence and dependence. Giving unsolicited advice implies that the recipient does not have the ability to make his or her own decisions. The facilitator may of course give advice if asked, but it is more helpful to assure the processor that he or she knows what is best for him- or herself.

Acting as a facilitator can be stressful and the facilitator shouldn't neglect his or her own needs. Sometimes what the processor uncovers may trigger strong emotions in the facilitator. The facilitator needs to deal with these emotions and nurture him or herself. If the facilitator is not comfortable with the situation, he or she must say so directly. If the facilitator and the processor have agreed to act as facilitators for each other, they should make sure each gets equal time to use the Process.

5

Uncover Hidden Parts
of Your Mind

You gain strength, courage and confidence by every experience in which you really stop to look fear in the face. You are able to say to yourself, 'I lived through this horror. I can take the next thing that comes along.' You must do the thing you think you cannot do.

—Eleanor Roosevelt

Sometimes when you cannot immediately access memories, it's because they are contained in other parts of your mind—parts you created to handle overwhelming trauma. If you feel that there are memories or emotions you cannot reach, ask yourself gently, while you are still in a state of relaxation, if there is another part of you that has these memories or emotions. The answer may be a clear yes or no, or just a sense that such a part exists. If you suspect that you have these hidden parts of your mind, you probably do, since most people have them. Therapists sometimes refer to these parts as *ego states*.

At times people may be consciously aware of these parts. Have you ever said or heard someone say, "Part of me wants to try it, but part of me is afraid"? Or "The child in me wants to play, but my parent part is telling me I should work"? We frequently talk about different "parts" of our minds. The theory of *transactional analysis* or *T.A.*, a popular type of therapy, is based on the mind having various child, adult, and parent ego states.

A trend toward recognizing that we all have various parts or multiple personalities is growing in many fields of study. In "Our Multiple Selves," Dr. Richard Schwartz offers this view: "Researchers at the cutting edge of psychoneurology, computer science, and artificial intelligence are converging on a new, multi-self view of people. In Ornstein's words, 'we are not a single person. We are many.' From this multi-self perspective, we no longer have to fear "fragmenting"—we are already fragmented. In a sense we are all multiple personalities. The condition we call multiple personality disorder only represents an extremely disengaged and polarized version of the ordinary operation of our internal system. This is a very difficult proposition for most people to fully accept, but once it is accepted one's view of one's self and of human nature is profoundly altered."

Why Your Mind Creates Ego States

Researchers believe that infants innately possess a number of states of consciousness. If an infant is subjected to trauma, a portion of his consciousness may be isolated from the whole, walled off to protect the greater consciousness from something it is too immature to process. This defense may be used very early in life, and memories from a very early age, even inside the womb, can be recovered. I created an ego state when I was in an incubator after my premature birth because my feelings of loneliness and abandonment were so devastating. I was born in 1941, before parents were allowed to touch infants in incubators. As an adult I had to make this infant part of me feel loved in order to rid myself of recurring painful feelings of loneliness and isolation.

Adults who were adopted have discovered parts only days old that contain the pain of losing their birth mothers and the love they and their mothers shared in the womb. And many people, including myself, have recovered memories of trauma in the womb. In fact, conscious connected breathing, a technique for releasing emotions at a deep level, which some psychiatrists now call holotropic breath work, used to be called rebirthing because therapists found it released trauma that occurred during the birth process. You can learn this technique on pages 103.

After the anguish of being squeezed out of the birth canal, newborn infants used to be yanked from their mothers with forceps, slapped to make them breathe, subjected to examinations by a doctor or nurse, and separated from their mothers in nurseries. Even though procedures today are somewhat more humane, the shock of even so-called natural childbirth is still substantial because the baby is forced from the comfort and security of the womb into a very different world. Some psychologists believe that our fear of Armageddon, of the world ending, comes from feelings during birth when our secure world ended. These feelings, and others during the preverbal stage, may come out during the Inner Exploration Process or during breath work.

Once your mind learns to create ego states and wall off painful feelings as a coping mechanism, it will continue to use this defense throughout your life—until you learn to handle your emotions consciously as they arise. You may even continue to create new parts to protect you from painful feelings as an adult. People who repeatedly block their feelings have few or no emotions; they are like the "walking dead." Although they are numb to painful emotions, they are also dead to feelings of joy and love.

Most people are frightened of uncovering these parts of their minds because they are afraid they will not be able to handle the emotions they suppressed. But the fact is that whatever happened to you, you have already survived it, including the emotions, and probably at a time when you were a child and truly helpless and vulnerable. Your mind protected you then, and will continue to protect you now. Feeling the old emotions will not kill you; it will set you free. Once you are able to feel and release your emotions as they arise, your mind will stop creating new parts.

At various times in your life, you may have been aware of thoughts and feelings surfacing from these hidden parts. Have you ever been aware of overreacting to a situation when you knew that your emotional response was way out of proportion to the event? A part of your mind containing strong repressed feelings may have been triggered and these old emotions made your present reaction more intense.

Have you ever had a thought that did not seem to be part of your stream of consciousness, an angry or weird thought that seemed to materialize from somewhere else? It may have come from a subconscious part of your mind. Some people with more extreme forms of dissociation may hear voices which come from severely wounded parts of their minds. If you hear voices that seem to come from outside your mind, you can be healed, but you should see a therapist to prevent you from becoming confused.

Encountering parts of yourself that you did not know existed can be scary because they seem to have minds of their own, but you can deal with them. All of these parts can be healed, no matter how destructive, angry, wounded, or complex they appear to be. Your mind created them in order to protect you, and you have ultimate control over all parts of your mind. (In some instances, sadistic organized cults may torture people to split their minds and program parts to do their bidding. Even in those cases where parts have been artificially created, they can be deprogrammed and healed.)

Getting to Know Your Hidden Parts

It is essential to find out as much about each ego state as possible. The more frightening a situation seems, the more important it is to get as much information as you can. I learned that where there is fear there is illusion. When you discover the truth about what happened to you and why your ego states were created, your fear will diminish through understanding. Part of me decided when I was a child that it was not safe to be happy. When I uncovered the memories this part contained, I found many instances where I had been playing as a child and my father, who was a writer, would become enraged and beat me because I was making noise and disturbing his work. I assumed that he did not want me to be happy, and my mind created an ego state to keep me from being happy by destroying any happiness I felt. I found that this ego state was responsible for sabotaging relationships, jobs I enjoyed, and other experiences of happiness. It would even put fearful thoughts in my mind when I started to enjoy something. I had to convince this part that its actions were counterproductive; my father was dead and there was now no reason to destroy my happiness—no one would punish me for being happy. It was difficult to face the fact that I had been preventing myself from being happy, but once I was able to heal this ego state, my life became much easier and much more enjoyable.

Sometimes your present fear may come from terror you felt and suppressed as a child. Once you recover the memory of your childhood event and release the old fear, the feeling will disappear. Each time you face your fears and the reasons for them, you will find it easier to uncover and heal other parts. Knowing yourself requires becoming aware of all parts of your mind and healing their wounds.

Self-awareness is liberating. When you find out more about parts of your mind, where they originate and what happened to you, you will discover that reactions and behavior you thought were irrational have a logical explanation. For example, I felt guilty as far back as I could remember because I hated my mother and did not know why. I thought I was a terrible person because I did not love my own mother. Only when I began to recover my repressed memories did I realize that my mother had known that my father was abusing me and did not stop him or take me away. After I released my feelings of rage and hatred, I began to understand my mother's actions and have compassion for her. I learned that she had also been abused as a child and realized she was trapped in a pattern of victimization and low self-esteem that made her unable to confront my father. I was then able to forgive her—and to love her. We were finally able to have a loving relationship and shared wonderful times together for several years before she died.

Recovering memories does not have to tear families apart. Disclosing the truth about family problems can lead to healing. It is our subconscious feelings of anger and hatred that keep us from being close and feeling love. Only through awareness of the truth can forgiveness and real feelings of love arise. When we accept and understand our own feelings, we develop compassion for other people. Healing our pasts eliminates the barriers that make us feel separate, different, and alone, improving all of our relationships by creating the opportunity for real intimacy.

It is important to keep in mind that *all* of your ego states were created to protect you. No matter how angry, hateful, or misguided a mind-part seems to be, it helped you survive and its purpose was to protect you. (The only exceptions are ego states deliberately created and programmed by someone else, usually members of sadistic cults). As you explore your various parts, you will find that each one has a reason for being there. With understanding and compassion, all parts can be healed, no matter how hurt or hostile they appear to be. Even if a part may want to kill you or everyone in the world, it can still be healed. I had a part that hated everyone and wanted to destroy the world because no one protected me when I was being abused or believed me when I asked for help. The amount of rage I discovered terrified me. But after I released the deep level of rage through the Inner Exploration Process and breath work, that part of me no longer had any destructive desires and was ready to be integrated. More miraculous was the fact that my uncontrollable temper was now controllable. I no longer reacted angrily to situations that used to provoke rage.

Keep in mind that these ego states are not separate entities. Even though at times they may seem as though they have minds of their own, they are still parts of your own mind—you created them. They may argue with you, but you probably have been conscious of arguing with yourself at times, of being "of two minds" about something before. This is similar, except that when you argue with an ego state you are usually arguing with a child who is unable to reason as an adult. You need to treat all your mind-parts as hurt children—listen to their stories and allow them to release their feelings. Keeping painful events from your conscious mind is a heavy burden, one that your ego states want to unload. What they want most is to let go of the secrets they contain. Since their purpose is to help you, they can be convinced to give up destructive beliefs and behaviors. You will find that some of these ego states have amazing power to sabotage your happiness. After you heal these ego states, you can sometimes convince them to use this power in positive ways, such as helping you find opportunities for success and happiness or helping you pick healthy partners and warning you to stay away from people who will hurt you.

Although you are now an adult, these parts of your mind were walled off when you were a child and never had a chance to grow up. They are still frightened children who may lash out in rage or act destructively because they are hurt. But if you treat them as the wounded children they are, with compassion and understanding, they will respond very quickly. They are starving for love, and as an adult, you have the power to give it to them. I found that what my mind-parts really wanted was to tell their stories, release their pain, and be at peace.

Over the centuries, saints, mystics, gurus, and more recently therapists have used techniques similar to the Inner Exploration Process for obtaining self-knowledge and enlightenment. However, in past centuries people did not understand psychology and thought that the angry, hurt parts of themselves and the voices they heard in their heads were "demons." Now we know that they are simply parts of our minds that have been walled off by trauma. They are the child parts of ourselves that need to be revealed and allowed to tell what they suffered so they can release their pain and rage.

If you have studied Eastern religions, you may have heard of *samskaras,* the karmic patterns that are said to control our lives. In *Freedom from the Bondage of Karma,* Swami Rama describes them this way: "Samskaras are the dormant traces of our past karmas, actions, thoughts, desires and memories. . . . Our samskaras, having all the potential of past memories, thoughts and deeds, remain latent in our subconscious mind. It is the subconscious mind which is the vehicle in which the soul travels from this place of life to another place. . . . As long as the soul uses the subconscious mind . . . we cannot become free of our karma at all." Some people have uncovered what they believe to be past-life memories using the Inner Exploration Process and the experiences they describe are similar to those of people who uncover parts containing memories from this life. Whatever you may believe about past lives, psychologists and spiritual teachers seem to agree that you must bring subconscious memories to consciousness.

These subconscious memories determine our personalities and how we react to present events; they govern our actions and what we experience in this life. I described the repressed parts that contain these memories to Swami Nogeshand, an American yogi, and he said they seemed to be what yogis call samskaras. Paramahansa Yogananda, an Indian saint, writes in *Autobiography of a Yogi* (the most transformational book I have found): "Identifying himself with a shallow ego, man takes for granted that it is he who thinks, wills, digest meals, and keeps himself alive, never admitting . . . that in his ordinary life he is naught but a puppet of past actions (karma) and of Nature or environment. Each man's intellectual reactions, feelings, moods, and habits are merely the effects of past causes, whether of this or a prior life." I believe from my own experience that by clearing these parts of our mind, we clear our past karma, and our lives change dramatically for the better.

All of your ego states need to be reeducated and healed, not eliminated. Your mind created each part to protect you and each had important functions; they are part of your mind, part of your experience. You have to become aware of them and heal them. Healing does not come by destroying any part of your mind. Every part has to be understood and accepted. The goal is to become aware of all of your ego states and clear them so that they are no longer subconscious and can no longer affect you without your conscious knowledge. When these parts are brought totally to consciousness, the memories they contain can finally be processed and integrated into other conscious information. Therapists call this process *integration.*

Instructions for Healing Ego States

The following instructions are to be used with the basic Inner Exploration Process when you are unable to uncover memories or information. Begin by gently asking yourself if there is a part that contains the memories or information. You will feel in your mind or body an answer or sense of whether such a part exists. Sometimes ego states contain visual or sensory memories, sometimes a particular emotion. If something overwhelming occurred when you were very young or if an event was prolonged or particularly traumatic, your mind may have created many different parts to deal with the events and the numerous emotions you felt. I found four different parts that contained memories and emotions of one abusive event.

If you sense that you have such parts, the next step is to convince yourself and your parts that you want to hear their stories and that you can handle the memories and feelings now. Ask your hidden parts to come out and talk to you in your mind. Provide reassurance and talk to these parts the way you would to a frightened child. Be honest—your subconscious always knows the truth anyway—and tell your child self how you feel, even if you are angry with him or her or are scared.

These parts of your mind are still childlike and may have been isolated from the parts of your mind that have grown up with you, so you cannot assume that they know what you know or can reason like an adult. Assure your parts that they do not need to protect you anymore, that you can deal with whatever happened, and that they can now release their burden of secrecy. You must convince each part that you want to get to know him or her and that you want to work together so you both can heal. Tell your parts that you can take care of them, that you are no longer helpless, and you now have the intelligence, strength, and ability to handle painful past experiences.

Ask each part what you need to do to make that part feel safe enough to release information and feelings to you, and do whatever is needed. When the part is convinced it is safe to let you have the memories, you will feel a shift in your mind and even in your body. Then ask your mind to bring you closer to the part of you that contains the memories, information, or emotions you need to recover now.

Some people have almost totally walled themselves off from painful feelings. After trying this technique, a talented designer in her early fifties described what she found this way: "It feels like I'm on the outside of a wall. I can feel the wall, it's brick. I put it up brick by brick." Each "brick" was a separate part of her mind that needed to be brought to conscious awareness.

If you have difficulty reaching your hidden parts, you can program your mind to allow them to come out. When you are in bed, before you go to sleep at night and in the morning after you awaken, simply tell yourself that you are ready to recover any memories you may have suppressed and that you now have the ability to handle them. Direct your mind to prepare you to recover memories and ask any part that is ready to come out and give you information. You might even set a deadline in your mind and tell yourself that you'll be ready to contact some parts in a week, or whatever time feels right for you. You have control of your mind and you can usually meet the deadlines you set.

Another helpful technique is to direct your parts to give you information through your dreams. Before you go to sleep, tell your mind that you would like to recover some memories in your dreams. Keep a pad by your bed so you can write down all the details of your dream as soon as you wake up. Think about the dream and record any thoughts you have about it. Read over what you have written later that day and consider what your mind is trying to tell you.

What to Do When You Discover a Part

When a part comes out and talks to you in your mind, through thoughts, pictures, or feelings, first ask how old it is—how old you were when it was created.

Next ask if the part has a name or something it would like to be called. Some parts may be you at various ages and have no other name; sometimes they may have specific names, nicknames, or call themselves by the primary emotion they contain. I had parts of various ages, as well as one that called itself "Hate," which contained that feeling to protect me from it.

You may want to find out if the part is male or female. Most will be the same sex as you, but sometimes parts may be another sex because they felt the other sex was stronger, less vulnerable, or had other qualities they wanted. This does not mean you are homosexual; we all have male and female aspects. Your mind may have copied someone you thought had a power or traits you lacked. This is simply another way your creative mind used to protect you from intensely painful feelings and events.

Ask the part why it was created. Every part has a purpose. The most common purposes are to protect your conscious mind from feelings that were overwhelming at the time and to insulate you from experiencing further pain. In cases of prolonged, repeated abuse, one part may replace another, the way you replace a new computer disk when it cannot hold any more memory. In some cases, parts may deal with particular forms of trauma, or life situations like doing schoolwork or dealing with friends.

Most people have many different mind-parts. Sometimes after uncovering several parts, you may think you have found them all. However, over the course of several years, I kept finding more parts and deeper levels of emotion. I often became discouraged and thought I would never be able to heal all of my mind-parts. But I did, others have, and so can you. Your subconscious mind knows how to heal all of your mind-parts.

If you cannot immediately discover a part's purpose, ask the part to let you have some of the memories it contains. You may see pictures, feel feelings, or simply have a sense of what happened. Obtain as much information and detail as possible. You will find that you can control how you recover memories. Although you need to recover the facts and feelings, you can speed up your experience of the memories or slow them down like a movie. Ask your mind to take you through painful memories as rapidly as possible while still providing the information you need to heal. Your mind knows how to do this.

Of course, you can stop whenever you want. It is important not to overwhelm yourself, especially the first few times you use the Inner Exploration Process. Once I felt comfortable using the Process, I tried to discover all the information I could about an event so I would not have to come back to that memory. But many times, my mind returned to the same memories and I recovered more details and deeper emotions.

The objective is to help each part release all of the information and all of the feelings it possesses at a pace that is safe for you. Some people like to take it slowly; others like to get it all out as quickly as possible. But if you begin to feel distressed to the point that you cannot conduct your daily activities, stop and seek professional help.

Sometimes a part will be willing to give you some information, but not the whole story all at once. Respect the part's wishes and help the child part feel safe with the process before you attempt to go further. You need to be a loving, gentle parent to every child part for this technique to work—and for you to learn to love yourself and heal.

Overwhelming emotions created your parts, and sometimes it is difficult to access those emotions. Your child parts may cling to their desire to protect you, afraid that you will find the emotions overwhelming. They need to be convinced that you can handle the memories and emotions now.

To release your feelings, go deeply into them and feel them as intensely as possible. Express them fully and out loud. Let the feelings flow through you without stopping them. Relive the situation as vividly as you can. Stay with the feelings until you feel an inner shift or until the emotions have been exhausted.

How to Uncover and Change Each Part's Self-Defeating Decisions

As in the basic Inner Exploration Process, make sure that you uncover all the decisions each part made about yourself, others, God, and the universe. Then change the decisions while you are still mentally experiencing the memory. People often discover parts that, although well-intentioned, contain beliefs that prevent the people from having what they want most. As children, these people may have made some destructive decisions: never to love anyone again because someone they loved hurt them; never to be happy because something awful happened when they were happy; never to be successful because they did not want an abusive parent to be proud of them; or never to be thin or attractive because they might be molested again. The list of possibilities is endless. I found dozens of parts containing destructive decisions that were sabotaging my life. It is a shock to find that our own unconscious beliefs control our lives and prevent us from being happy. But accepting this truth is the beginning of accepting responsibility for our lives—and real healing.

I have seen very clearly that the universe is benevolent, and that we are surrounded by infinite abundance. Love, spirituality, and beauty are everywhere, but we do not see them because our unconscious beliefs make us blind. We are supposed to be happy and enjoy the blessings of life, but we push away what we want because of our unconscious beliefs.

After you have changed a part's negative decisions and released all of the emotions, ask the part if there is anything else it needs in order to be totally healed—and provide it. Then ask if the part is ready to be integrated, to be an unseparated part of your mind. If the part says yes, and you *feel* that the part is ready, send the part love and welcome it into your heart. If a part reappears, it means that some other aspect still needs to be healed.

Every one of your mind-parts has much to teach you about your past and about yourself. It helps if you can see your parts as gifts, protectors who have suffered much pain to spare you unbearable distress. My therapist always thanked my mind-parts whenever she talked to them and I learned to follow her example. When I began to see the horror my ego states hid from me so that I could grow up and function, I was overwhelmed with gratitude.

Exploring yourself can be an exciting and challenging task. You may find it difficult to accept this viewpoint when you are overcome by pain and despair. But if you can recognize the creative and effective ways your mind protected you when you needed it most, you will be able to thank yourself for your intelligence and your strength.

I believe that accepting, healing, and integrating parts of the mind is a metaphor for accepting, healing, and integrating all of the people in the world. We have much to learn from all the parts of our minds.

6

Using the Process to Find Your Real Self and Inner Happiness

There is a spark of good in everybody, no matter how deeply it may be buried. It is the real you. When I say 'you' what am I really thinking of? Am I thinking of the clay garment, the body? No, that's not the real you. Am I thinking of the self-centered nature? No, that's not the real you. The real you is that divine spark.

—Peace Pilgrim

The greatest discovery I made during my own healing was that the wonderful, essentially good part of me, which had existed from my earliest moments of consciousness, was still alive and untainted by later, painful experiences. I made this discovery one day by chance. I was using the Inner Exploration Process by myself at home when I recalled a new, particularly gruesome memory. I was overwhelmed by horror, fear, and anger. My therapist and I had assumed that most of the worst memories had come out, but I continued to find more. I was sick and tired of spending time uncovering awful memories. I remember thinking that there must have been some time in my life when I was happy. All of a sudden it occurred to me that if my mind could go back to awful events, I should also be able to retrieve memories of happy times.

Returning to a relaxed state, I asked my mind to take me back to a time when I was happy. In a few moments I began to feel a wonderful bubbly feeling, as though my body were filled with thousands of tiny champagne bubbles. My body felt light, totally free of pain and anxiety. I was outdoors, lying on my back on a blanket in the sunshine, playing with my toes. I was less than two years old.

The feelings of joy and peace were extraordinary, incredibly different from the inner anguish that was the norm for me. I could not conceive of anything but love. I had no thoughts of being bad, or damaged, or inadequate. I simply basked in the sensations of the sunshine, and the curiosity of exploring the way my toes moved. I wanted to stay in that memory forever and tried to memorize what it felt like to be happy. Coming back to the heaviness and anxiety of my adult world was a terrible jolt.

I mentally returned to that memory many times to train my mind and body to get into the habit of feeling happiness. I also retrieved other early childhood memories of what I was like when the abuse started. I remembered a time when I found my mother crying because she knew my father was sexually abusing me. I saw myself trying to climb on to her lap to comfort her and make her feel better, but she pushed me away. That memory made me realize how much love I possessed as a child. My mother knew what my father was doing to me and *I* was still trying to comfort *her*, when I needed so much to be comforted and protected myself. I was amazed by my compassion and my desire to heal my mother's pain, in spite of my own.

Recovering these memories helped me wipe out my conviction that because I was abused, I must have been a bad person. My memories showed me that all I wanted as a child was to love and be loved. When I realized that I was born good, I saw that the abuse had changed my *feelings* but it had not changed *me*. The loving, innocent part of me was still alive—and that was my true self. My abuse did not kill it. It was the real me. My painful, violent feelings were just an illusory shroud surrounding my essential core, my soul. That core could not be violated. Whatever my parents did to my mind and body, my soul remained untouched.

One of the greatest benefits of the Inner Exploration Process is that you can use it to recover happy memories and experience your true self, the self that existed before you were hurt and believed lies about yourself. Your pain, anger, and defenses have been like a shroud or a veil that covers your true self. But you can get in touch with the joyful, loving, innocent part of yourself, the real child who still lives inside you. This is who you really are, not just an imaginary inner child. Many people are afraid that the happy, loving child inside them was destroyed, or that were never happy or loving. But everyone has this core, it is our true selves and can never be destroyed. It may be deeply buried, but it survives no matter what is done to you and no matter what you do. You can always rediscover it. Your subconscious mind has recorded every event and sensation you experienced so that all of your memories are always part of you, the happy ones as well as traumatic ones.

I believe Jesus was referring to this idea when he said, "Except ye . . . become as little children, ye shall not enter into the kingdom of heaven." He also said the kingdom of heaven is inside us. Since Jesus experienced the pain of being human, he must have understood how this core can become buried under pain. I believe he was telling people to rediscover their original child self so they can experience the joy and peace of heaven that is their birthright.

You can go back in your mind to reexperience that loving, happy part, and once you actually feel what it is like, you can bring those feelings forward into the present. If you repeat this technique often, you may find that the sensations begin to become habitual, and your actions will come from this loving self. Then your future will change dramatically.

I strongly recommend that you use the Inner Exploration Process several times to uncover painful events before using it to uncover your core self. This is because the experience of discovering your core self will be more powerful after you understand the pain you have suffered and why you feel the way you do now. The comparison will be more dramatic and will have a greater impact, psychologically and spiritually. This technique is much more than simply thinking consciously about a happy time. When you are really relaxed and allow your own mind to select a memory for you, you will feel the sensations not just in your mind but in your body. Then you will be able to see clearly who you were before painful experiences caused you to forget.

I frequently helped clients experience their core selves at the end of therapy sessions in which they had discovered deep negative beliefs or particularly destructive parts and had experienced intense anger, grief, and hatred. Understanding who they really were enabled them to accept their violent emotions and the hurtful parts of themselves because they knew that their happy, loving core existed underneath. Once you experience this child part that is always pure and free from stress, your life will be transformed.

The Technique

The steps for using this technique are the same as for the basic Inner Exploration Process. Sit comfortably, close your eyes, and take a few deep, slow breaths. Use the progressive relaxation exercise on page 149, meditation, or any other technique that helps you relax.

When you feel deeply relaxed, simply ask your mind to take you back to a memory of a time when you were truly happy. Mentally tell yourself to go back as far as you have to go to find such a memory. Avoid forcing anything, or anticipating what memory will arise. You may repeat the instruction to yourself as necessary.

If you are trying too hard or guessing what will come up, picture something pleasant in your mind—a flower or a sunset—or use a mantra to clear your mind of tension. Simply allow a memory to float up into your mind. Give it time; the right memory will come.

When a happy memory comes, just stay with it, observing how it feels in your mind and body. Let the pleasurable feelings flow throughout your body for as long as possible. Memorize how it feels to be completely happy. Observe every detail. What does your body feel like? How does your mind feel? Notice what thoughts you have about yourself, other people, and the universe. Imagine what your life would be like if you felt this way all the time. How you would talk, dress, walk, interact with other people?

Don't worry if you cannot immediately recall a memory of happiness, or if you stumble on an unpleasant memory. It simply means that you have some issues to work out before retrieving happy memories. Conscious and unconscious negative beliefs about yourself and feelings that you do not deserve happiness can prevent you from uncovering happy memories. But even if the happy, loving part of you is deeply buried, it is still there. We were all born loving, and that part of you is still alive.

For some people happiness may be so unfamiliar that they are afraid of it or believe they don't deserve it. A client I will call Carol was neglected by her parents and molested by a neighbor. When she took her mind back to a happy time, she described feeling warm and loved, cradled in her mother's arms while her mother rocked and sang to her in a rocking chair. She kept repeating with a joyful awe, "My mother really loved me."

I told Carol to stay with the memory and enjoy the feeling. Suddenly her face and body contorted with fear. I asked her what was happening, and her little girl voice replied: "Claws are tearing apart my memory. Something evil is destroying it."

Her fear was contagious and for a moment I wondered how to cope with it. I told Carol that she had control of her mind and that some fear or belief was destroying her memory, not something outside of herself. I asked if there was a part of her mind that did not want her to be happy, and she found a part that thought she should have told about being molested as a child so that other children would not have been abused by the same man. When Carol realized that she had been too young to tell and too terrified by the threats of her molester, the "claws" disappeared. Carol was then able to return to the memory of her mother's love and her happy, innocent self.

Subconscious feelings of guilt or shame can prevent people from accessing memories of this happy, loving part. If you cannot find such a memory or start to have negative thoughts or feelings when you do, you need to uncover the part of your mind that feels unworthy to experience happiness. Use the Inner Exploration Process to heal that part and any others that may be sabotaging your happiness and then try this exercise again.

Everyone has memories of their true selves and you can recover yours, even if you have to mentally go all the way back into the womb to find one. Some people are doubtful of having memories from the womb, but many people have experienced such memories. Therapists who use rebirthing (the breathing technique on page 102), have witnessed people reliving memories in the womb and in many cases those memories were later confirmed by parents. Premature babies can be kept alive even if born only a few months after conception. Some have memories of being in incubators after birth. If they have such early memories after birth, why couldn't other children have memories while inside the womb at the same age?

Another client I will call Gwen had some conscious memories of brutal abuse by her father. She had used the Inner Exploration Process many times in our therapy sessions to recover other violent memories and was looking forward to retrieving happy ones. But despite being deeply relaxed, she was unable to find a single memory of joy or peace. As she took her mind further and further back, she became distressed and kept saying, "There is nothing. Nothing is there."

I became concerned that Gwen's expectations of finding her happy, loving part would be dashed and that she would be devastated. I said a prayer for guidance and then remembered that when I could not find the cause of a certain body memory during my own therapy, my therapist had told me to take my mind back into the womb where I had discovered the cause.

I took a deep breath and told Gwen to keep going back to a time when she felt safe and loved even if she had to go back into the womb. Nothing happened. I waited for several minutes, not knowing what to do. Then, slowly, Gwen's expression of anxiety relaxed into one of total peace. A smile transformed her mouth. The change was dramatic.

When I see signs that clients are recovering memories, I usually ask where they are, how old they are, and what they are seeing. I asked

Gwen these questions, but unlike our other sessions, she did not respond. Then I realized that if she were in the womb, she would not be able to talk, even though her adult mind could hear and understand what I was saying. So I asked her whether she could speak and told her to move her head to indicate "yes" or "no". Her head moved slightly from one side to the other.

I stopped asking questions and simply let Gwen enjoy whatever she was feeling. After a while, I reminded her that the way she was feeling was the way she was meant to feel. I also told her adult mind to analyze the memory and decide whether Gwen was a bad person. I suggested that she memorize her feelings and bring them back into the present.

When Gwen opened her eyes, she was radiant. She had a confidence and serenity I had not seen before. She said she knew she was in the womb and had experienced a total relaxation and peace she had not believed was possible; she knew without any doubt that she was perfect and so was everything else. Even after many discussions, Gwen had been unable to erase her lifelong belief that she was bad, a conclusion she reached because of her abuse and because her father repeatedly told her she was evil and deserved to be punished. But after feeling what she was like in the womb, she realized that she had always been good and knew that she was not responsible for what her father did.

Each time you find a happy memory, after you fully experience it, remember to tell yourself to bring the feelings back into the present. When you open your eyes, before getting up, do your best to feel the happiness and love in your mind and body. You may have to return to the memory several times before you are able to recreate the feelings at will. Hold on to those feelings as long as you can and remember them throughout the day.

You can go back to the happy memory you recovered, or find others, as often as you choose. Each time you do this exercise, you are training your mind and body to get into the habit of feeling happiness. The more you experience the sensation of happiness, the more effective the results will be. And the more you clear your past, the happier you will be— without trying. Feeling happy also stimulates your immune system and improves your overall health. Some people have even found that physical problems have disappeared after they used this technique over a period of time.

Be sure to try this technique again after you have used the Inner Exploration Process to clear out as many painful experiences and healed as many mind-parts as possible. What will be left after you clear your past is the real you—the clear you. I learned only recently, just as this book was going to press, that when we have truly cleared out the old pain and beliefs, we gain direct access to our real self and to extraordinary knowledge. A friend and exceptional therapist showed me that I could use this technique to ask my real self fundamental questions about life: where I came from, the nature of the universe and God, what my purpose here is, and how to achieve my mission. I simply asked my mind to show me the truth about myself, the universe, and why I was here. I was stunned to hear the answers that came out of my mouth; those answers were very different from what I had anticipated before I was in the relaxed state. Our minds really do contain all of the answers we need, including memories and information from our earliest moments of consciousness. I do not want to spoil your wonder and joy by describing the responses I received because each person's experience is unique and yours will be perfect for you. I can only assure you that if you use this technique to question your real self, after you have done your best to clear out your self-defeating emotions and beliefs, the results will be astounding.

Some people may be able to obtain answers to these fundamental questions without clearing all or most of their pasts, but these truths usually will not be revealed until past issues are resolved. As long as you have unhealed ego states or are repressing painful experiences, you may receive unreliable or confusing answers from hurt or angry parts of your mind. If the answers you receive are negative, critical, or produce fear, they are not coming from your real self. Answers from your real self bring peace and joy. Your real self will also have a sense of humor; mine told me to stop being so serious.

I can see that I was not ready to receive these truths until now. I wouldn't have believed the answers, might have misinterpreted them, and certainly would not have known what to do about them. I had to change my view of the universe, people, and myself before I was ready for the knowledge I received. Although I had heard and read somewhat similar things from other sources, the effect of hearing them from myself made everything fall into place for me.

This technique has such powerful results that if I had to choose only one technique to use for my psychological and spiritual healing, it would be this one. It taught me who we all really are and that we were created to be happy. Happiness, harmony, and love are our true nature.

7

Healing Physical Pain, Disease, and Injury

I thank God for my handicaps, for through them, I have found myself, my work, and my God.

—Helen Keller

The Inner Exploration Process has the ability to heal more than psychological and emotional conditions. The same technique can be used to uncover and heal the underlying causes of so-called physical conditions. Twenty years ago, I would not have believed that it was possible to heal pain, disease, and injury with my mind. I believed that such conditions were purely physical and could only be cured by physical treatments— traditional interventions used by Western physicians, such as pills, shots, and surgery. I had an experience that helped changed my views dramatically.

Throughout my life, I had been plagued by a seemingly endless number of gynecological problems. I now recognize these ailments as symptoms of childhood sexual abuse, but at the time I thought they were "just physical." A gynecologist had found two large cysts, one on each of my ovaries; one he described as the size of a Florida grapefruit and the other the size of a ripe tomato. He told me that ovarian cysts usually disappear by themselves, but when they grew as large as mine they were beyond the point of shrinking on their own and required surgery.

Having already undergone a couple of gynecological operations, I was reluctant to be cut up again and told my doctor I wanted to wait a few weeks to see if the cysts would shrink. He insisted that I return in three weeks and that if the cysts were still there, he would schedule the surgery.

I was terrified. At that time, I knew nothing about using mind power to heal, but I had heard somewhere that self-hypnosis could be used to shrink tumors. I purchased a paperback book on self-hypnosis and followed the instructions for relaxing. I learned that self-hypnosis is a natural state of relaxed concentration we all experience for fifteen or twenty minutes every two hours when we are awake. We have diurnal (or daytime) cycles that correspond to our nocturnal sleep cycles. We have fifteen or twenty minutes of rapid eye movement (REM) every two hours at night when we dream and process daily events and anxieties. We have similar cycles during the day when our minds need to rest and process information. During this time, our mind may wander, we may want to rest or stretch, and we may feel hungry. Psychologist Ernest Rossi, Ph.D., wrote a fascinating book called *The 20 Minute Break* about how we can use these periods to reduce stress, maximize performance, and improve health.

Milton Erickson, M.D., the acknowledged father of modern hypno-therapy, used these natural twenty-minute periods to help clients recover memories without hypnotizing them. He found that when people are relaxed and focused, they are able to obtain more information from their minds than when they are engaged in worry and constant activity. Contrary to the prevalent myths about hypnosis, hypnotized people remain alert and in control of their minds and bodies; no one can control them. I was relieved to find that I could come out of the state of relaxation any time I wanted and that I would not become a zombie as I had feared.

Although I did not really believe self-hypnosis would work, I spent fifteen or twenty minutes twice a day relaxing and mentally visualizing the cysts on my ovaries growing smaller. At the same time, I repeated in my mind, "My cysts are becoming smaller and smaller and disappear-ing." I didn't feel anything changing, but continued out of desperation.

When the gynecologist examined me three weeks later, he was clearly stunned and blurted out, "I don't understand this! What have you been doing?" From his shocked tone, I thought the cysts had grown larger or burst, and asked what was wrong. This gynecologist, who had been practicing for over forty years, said he'd never seen anything like it:

the cyst that had been the size of a grapefruit had shrunk to the size of a tomato, and the tomato-sized cyst was completely gone.

Although I was afraid he would ridicule me, I confessed that I had used self-hypnosis. To my surprise, he said that at the hospital where he operated, he had seen surgery performed using hypnosis in place of anesthesia, and that now he would believe anything. He told me to continue to do whatever I was doing. When I returned for an examination three weeks later, both cysts were gone.

I told this story to some of my friends who found it incredible, chalking up my healing to "spontaneous remission"—meaning they could find no explanation. I began to have doubts myself and forgot about using my mind for healing. But several years later, another crisis forced me to use it again.

This time I fell while skiing, twisting my knees so that my ski tips somehow became stuck in the snow. I was hanging in the air, and my ski bindings did not release, so I could not get down on the ground. Since it was a weekday in late spring, there were very few skiers on the mountain. My friends had skied on ahead of me and were nowhere in sight. I was in excruciating pain and had to wrench my knees even more to lower myself to the ground where I remained sobbing until my friends climbed back up to find me and called the ski patrol.

The ligaments in both knees were torn and one knee was swollen to the size of a football. The ski patrol splinted my legs, lay me in a sled, and strapped me down so they could tow me to the emergency clinic. Since I was in a remote area of the ski resort, they had to haul the sled up one part of the mountain by snowmobile and then pull the sled on skis down another part of the mountain, a maneuver that took almost an hour.

For the first ten minutes or so, I was in agony. Then I remembered my long-past experience with self-hypnosis. I didn't know whether or not it would work on the intense pain of torn ligaments, but I had nothing to lose by trying and nothing better to do as the sled bumped over the snow. I put myself into a relaxed state, no easy feat while strapped to a sled being bounced by a noisy snowmobile up a mountain, and simply told myself over and over that I felt no pain. To my amazement, as long as I remained relaxed and was able to repeat this affirmation, the pain disappeared.

However, the ski patrol had been trained to keep checking to make sure their passengers did not lose consciousness. Each time a patrolman stopped to ask me if I was all right, I was jarred out of my relaxed state of concentration and the pain returned. But as long as I was not interrupted, I was able to keep the pain away as we hurtled up and down the mountain, and even while my knee was being x-rayed in the clinic. The problem was that I could not keep myself in the relaxed state of concentration the whole time so the results were only temporary.

The doctors in the emergency clinic wanted to give me painkilling drugs, and ignored me when I told them I had been able to mentally stop the pain. They thought either I had an unusually high pain tolerance, although all my life I had been extremely sensitive to pain, or that I was in a state of shock. But I knew I had discovered something really significant.

I started experimenting with using my mind to heal all kinds of physical conditions—headaches, toothaches, stress, and illness. I found that I was able to use the Inner Exploration Process to uncover reasons for each of them and make them disappear, not just temporarily but permanently. But one success eclipsed them all.

All my life I had severe bronchitis at least once a year and each time had to stay in bed for a week and take a full course of antibiotics in order to recover. Eight years ago I tried the Inner Exploration Process when I had my annual bout of bronchitis and recovered memories that revealed powerful reasons for this recurring illness. I discovered that as a child when I was in bed with bronchitis, my father did not abuse me. And, even though she ignored the abuse, my mother took care of me when I was ill.

As soon as I understood these apparent benefits of having bronchitis, I was able to convince the child parts of my mind that my father could no longer abuse me because he was dead, and that illness did not protect me from adult challenges, but made them worse because I now had to take care of myself when I was sick. Once my child parts agreed that making me ill was no longer helpful, not only did the bronchitis disappear then, but I have never had another case of bronchitis since that time more than eight years ago.

Over the years, I found books and even doctors that confirmed my experiences of using the power of my mind to heal, and I finally became convinced our minds can affect our physical condition. I started asking some of my therapy clients if they would like to try the technique. At first we only used the process to relieve headaches and menstrual cramps. In each instance, the client was able to uncover a memory that immediately relieved the pain.

Then a client I will call Barbara telephoned to cancel an appointment because her back had gone into spasm the day before and she could not move. She said she had suffered from back spasms in the past that had always kept her in bed for six weeks. When Barbara mentioned that she had not been doing anything particularly strenuous at the time the spasm occurred, I was immediately intrigued and asked Barbara if someone could bring her to my office so we could try the Inner Exploration Process on her back spasm. I had been using the Process with Barbara to help her recover additional memories of having been sexually abused by her father to supplement the conscious memories she had when she started therapy, so she was familiar with the steps.

Barbara was somewhat skeptical about using the Process to heal her back spasm but was willing to try anything to avoid being flat on her back for six weeks. Barbara's husband drove her to my office and carried her in because she could not walk or stand by herself. After placing her on the couch, he left, saying he thought trying to use psychology to cure a back spasm was sheer nonsense. Barbara's body was doubled up and she was clearly in severe pain.

We started by discussing whether there was any problem Barbara was aware of consciously that could be causing her spasm or anything she might want to avoid doing. Barbara could not think of anything, so she proceeded to put herself into a state of relaxation. I then asked her mind to give her information or a memory of why she had the back spasm.

The first things that came up were images of difficulties Barbara had been having with a male professor, the head of her doctoral committee. This professor had been critical and demanding, and was angry with Barbara for not completing her thesis more quickly. Barbara felt so depressed by his disapproval that she had not worked on her dissertation for weeks. The thought came to Barbara that she "wanted him off her back," but was afraid to tell him.

She realized that her interactions with the professor had triggered early childhood feelings of not being good enough. But I felt there was more and asked if her mind could find any other reason for the back spasm. After several minutes of silence, Barbara became very distressed and experienced memories of her abusive father's constant criticism, sneering that Barbara was stupid and could never do anything right. Her father made it clear that he thought women were worthless, and Barbara believed women were weak and vulnerable because she could not protect herself from being raped by him. She recalled that, as a child, she had been immobilized by depression for long periods as a result of her father's verbal and sexual abuse.

Barbara immediately saw the similarity between her father's disapproval and unreasonable demands and her professor's behavior, but, using her adult mind, she was able to distinguish her professor's criticism from her father's violent abuse. She also saw the connection between her childhood feelings of worthlessness and helplessness and her adult feelings when her professor criticized her. She then began to understand how those feelings had triggered her deep childhood belief that women were useless and that she would never be good at anything. Although Barbara's child self hated her father and wanted him to "get off her back," Barbara was afraid to confront him because when she tried to fight her father, he hurt her more. This old fear also prevented her from confronting her professor. The reason Barbara had become immobilized by the back spasm was that her child self believed it was useless to do anything because whatever she did would never be good enough and because she was afraid to stand up for herself.

Barbara worked through her feelings of fear and anger at her father and was able to change her self-defeating beliefs. She convinced her child self that she had to have been exceptionally intelligent and strong to survive what her father had done and that the child part no longer had to protect Barbara by immobilizing her to avoid disappointment and failure. Barbara was then also able to acknowledge that she could "do things right" because she had graduated from college with honors, passed the oral exams for her doctorate at a major Ivy League college, and was now teaching at a university. She also recognized the possibility that her professor was genuinely concerned about her finishing her degree and said that now she would be able to talk to him and negotiate a new deadline.

I again asked if there was anything else, and Barbara said she felt clear. She opened her eyes and *sat up!* She described the pain in her back as being "much less" and when her husband came to pick her up, she walked to the car with only a little help from him. Two days later Barbara called and said the back spasm was completely gone. She had also started to work on her dissertation again.

Since that time I have seen many cases where clearing out memories of painful childhood events has healed so-called physical conditions, diseases, and injuries. While I always advise people to continue the treatment prescribed by their physicians, I believe augmenting this treatment with the Inner Exploration Process is essential to achieving wellness. I have seen so many astounding recoveries when people uncover the psychological causes of their conditions that these recoveries have begun to seem ordinary rather than miraculous. There are a growing number of chiropractors and other healers who use neuro-emotional techniques to program injuries and disabling diseases out of people's bodies.

Psychiatrist Milton Erickson discovered the power of self-hypnosis as a teenager when he was paralyzed by polio from the neck down. His doctors said he would never leave his bed. Erickson refused to believe the doctors and began using his mind to concentrate on a single finger for hours each day, willing it to move. His concentration took him into a natural state of relaxation, what some call a self-hypnotic trance state. After several months, he was able to move his finger, and later his whole upper body. Erickson saw clearly the power of the mind-body connection and went to medical school to become a psychiatrist so that he could use what he learned about self-hypnosis to heal others—mentally *and* physically.

Yogis and Buddhist monks have used techniques similar to the Inner Exploration Process for centuries to uncover the roots of anger, unwelcome thoughts, and disease. Vietnamese Buddhist priest Thich Nhat Hanh describes a breathing process taught by his monastic order that focuses awareness on emotions and uncovers the underlying causes of anger. And Swami Satyananda Saraswati of the Bihar School of Yoga in India has written about how modern psychology and neurobiological discoveries support the use of various ancient meditation techniques to uncover damaging core beliefs and patterns in ways similar to the Inner Exploration Process. This knowledge has been around for ages, but people in the West have ignored it. You do not have to go to a guru or an expensive psychiatrist to clear your past; you simply have to take the time to go inside your own mind.

The Technique

Over the years, I refined the Inner Exploration Process for use specifically with physical conditions. While the basic process is the same, there are a couple of additional components for healing pain and other physical ailments. I found it helpful to use my mind to go deeply into the feeling of pain or discomfort. Instead of pushing away pain, I try to intensify it, to make it as strong as I can; at the same time I direct my mind to go more and more deeply into the pain. I allow whatever is there to be there, without resistance, no matter how uncomfortable the pain becomes. It is as though I am searching for the point where the pain originates, the center or focus—the most powerful spot. Often the pain moves around, changing location and intensity as I focus on it. This phenomenon has done much to convince me that pain and disease are psychological because the symptoms do not stay in one place. As the pain moves, I use my mind to follow the pain or other symptoms, going deeper and deeper inside them, always seeking the source.

I continue to stay deep inside the pain or discomfort, feeling it as intensely as possible, while I ask my mind to give me information or a memory to explain why the pain is there. Once an image, thought, or memory arises in my mind, I follow the steps of the Inner Exploration Process to obtain as much information and detail as possible, release old emotions, and uncover all the negative conclusions I reached based on the situation. If I discover parts of my mind that are responsible for the pain or disease, I reassure and heal them (as described in chapters 2 and 5), making every effort to convince them to give up their dysfunctional way of protecting me and to take on a more helpful role.

I continue to focus on the area of pain, mentally diving inside of it, while I work on changing my self-defeating conclusions. Frequently, after concentrating on staying deep inside the pain for several moments, I will feel a physical release in my body, a jerk or some other sensation that seems to expel the pain or condition.

Sometimes it helps to repeat to myself the negative statements that were causing the pain. I do this even after I have rejected the conclusions, in order to recreate more strongly the original emotions. This seems to help trigger the release mechanism in my body. Experiment with various ways of using your mind to determine what works best for you.

Different people experience different sensations of release, but it is generally a physical shift. You will know it when it happens. Usually your pain or other condition will be gone or substantially reduced. One woman described her experience as going into her pain with her mind and "popping it out." She said that when she went really deeply into the pain, she would experience a pop in the painful area and the pain would vanish. Another woman found that when she focused on areas of discomfort and simply stayed focused, allowing the discomfort to simply be there without resisting or judging it, her body would begin to move on its own into various positions. She described the movements as similar to what a chiropractor might do. When these movements ceased, the pain and discomfort were gone, even though she did not recover any conscious memories of the cause.

Some people find it helpful to send love to their pain or disease. This technique has worked for me: I simply ask my mind to send love to the area of discomfort and visualize comforting it while I touch the area gently with my hand. Sometimes I picture white light coming into my head and body and focus the light on the distressed area. I remind myself that my body is merely atoms and particles spinning around, actually more than 90 percent space. Our cells are holograms of perfection, so anything less than perfect is an illusion. I also pray for help in healing myself.

I believe that these methods work because when we use our minds to focus our attention on areas of conflict and stress, we activate the innate healing power of our minds. By concentrating on these areas, we are able to expose the underlying causes of distress. The act of concentrating on distressed areas with a positive intent also seems to release healing energy that helps bring us back to our natural state of wholeness.

I have not found it helpful to try to fight pain or disease, or to visualize cutting it out with a knife, because it is literally self-defeating to fight, kill, or throw out any part of ourselves. The key to healing is self-acceptance. As strange as it may seem, pain, illness, or injury is there to protect or help in some way, and its purpose is to foster psychological and spiritual growth.

Physicians who use mental techniques to cure cancer patients have found that images of fighting generally do not work as well as more positive images. Several years ago, these doctors used to direct children to visualize battling their disease with swords or guns, but discovered that visualizations such as Pac-man eating the diseased cells and becoming stronger were more effective. Many doctors now advise their cancer patients to make friends with their disease, acknowledging the ancient truth that love really does conquers all.

When I first used the Inner Exploration Process for physical conditions, it took me over an hour, sometimes two or three to release pain or relieve other conditions. However, as I worked with the Process, I could do it faster and am now able to release most pain and stress in less than fifteen minutes.

What If the Pain or Condition Returns?

If your pain or physical condition returns, it may be because you have not resolved all of the underlying issues and you may need to use the Inner Exploration Process again. In a couple of instances, I had to uncover more than a dozen different memories and negative beliefs over a period of months before the condition would release and I was finally completely free of it.

Sometimes, even though you have resolved all of your old issues, a pain or condition may recur at a later time, and you may discover a new issue in your present life that is causing the problem. Clearing out your past does not mean you will be free of stress and challenges forever. It simply means you will not be burdened by old baggage and that your present reactions will not be blown out of proportion by emotions you have stuffed. As long as you are alive, you will face challenges and stress; they are part of being human. But I can tell you from personal experience that new challenges are much easier to face if you are not weighed down by old ones you have not resolved.

Now, I sometimes use this quicker technique to rid my body of stress accumulated during the day: When I get into bed at night, I relax and imagine that the bed is dissolving and I am falling. I imagine Jesus or an angel catching me, so I feel safe and can relax totally. In a few moments, I usually feel the stressful areas jerk and release. It is now rarely necessary to go deeply into my places of stress, unless they are particularly stubborn.

Are there times when these techniques will not work, when disease will progress and we will die? Of course. Does this mean we have not tried hard enough, that we are not spiritual enough, or that we have somehow failed? Absolutely not. Death of the body is a natural part of the earthly life cycle. And I believe at some deep level we know when it is time to pass on.

But I have seen proof that if we heal our old mental wounds and clear our pasts, we will experience disease, pain, and death in a more positive way—without suffering and with joy. Our vision of the world changes and we become so aware of the miracles surrounding us that we barely notice the condition of our body. The Russian novelist Fyodor Dostoyevsky described this truth in a poignant scene in *The Brothers Karamazov* in which a nineteen year old boy confined to his bed and dying of tuberculosis talks to his mother:

> "Don't cry, mother, don't," he'd tell her. "I still have a long time to live and have a good time, for life is so good and so full of joy!"
>
> "How can it be such a joy to you, my darling, when you are so feverish at night and cough so that it sounds as if your chest is about to burst . . . ?"
>
> "Mother," he would answer, "don't be sad. Life is paradise; we all live in paradise, although we don't want to see it. As soon as we are willing to recognize it, the whole world will become a paradise; it could happen tomorrow, any time."

Part II

Other Techniques for Transforming Your Life

There are an infinite number of ways to gain greater understanding of our minds and to heal. There is no one "right" way. We are in a constant process of learning and growing; we are presented with lessons and insights every day, perhaps every moment. We can accelerate the growth process through conscious awareness and deliberate intention, by focusing on clearing our minds and taking advantage of the many techniques that are available to us. Although the Inner Exploration Process is the most effective technique I have found for clearing the mind at a deep and permanent level, I have also used many other helpful techniques during my own healing process and with my clients.

Most of these techniques have been used for decades by psychotherapists, and a few have been handed down for centuries by spiritual teachers. However, all of these techniques can be used without a psychotherapist or spiritual teacher. You can do them by yourself or to supplement your work with a therapist.

These techniques are designed for a variety of purposes, some specific, such as exercises for dealing with the death of a significant person in your life, and others more general, such as breathing technique for releasing emotions at a deep level. Exercises are included to help you understand yourself, improve your self-esteem, overcome depression, increase your confidence, nurture your inner child, relax, energize, change old thought patterns, calm your mind, live in the present moment, and have a happier more fulfilling life. It is not necessary to do all of these exercises. Read through the exercises and experiment with the ones you think or feel you need now, and keep in mind that the others are available when and if you need them.

Use what works for you. However, keep in mind that if you have a strong negative reaction to an exercise, it may be one you really need. You may want to complete some of the other exercises first and, when you feel stronger, come back to the ones that evoked negative feelings. Don't worry about doing it "right." Whatever you choose to do will be right for you and help you progress on your journey to recover your true self.

8

Coping with Feelings

You have the right to feel sad, betrayed, angry, and resentful when you've been injured. Understand, accept, and express your feelings. Pushing them below the surface only means they will erupt in another place, at another time.

—David W. Schell, D. Ed.,
Getting Bitter or Getting Better

The best way to deal with strong feelings is to let them out. The saying "What you resist persists" is especially true of emotions. We were created to have emotions and they are there for a purpose. Some people think we are only supposed to be loving, peaceful, and joyful all the time. Nonsense!

All of our emotions are important; they are part of being human. However, our culture frowns on expressions of emotion such as hatred and anger. But these emotions are necessary for survival and growth. Anger is an indication that something is wrong and needs attention. Hatred provides the strength to survive painful events. It is only when we stuff these emotions or act on them inappropriately that they become destructive. I tried for years to eliminate all feelings of anger until I heard the Dalai Lama, my model for an enlightened person, says he still becomes angry at times.

By releasing the old anger we have suppressed, we react with less anger in the present. The old rage most of us still carry may make us feel more anger than the present situation warrants, and when the old anger is triggered, we may act in hurtful ways. New studies indicate that we store emotions not just in our minds but in our bodies, and these old emotions cause stress and later dis-ease.

It is generally not necessary to express anger directly at the people who hurt or offend you, as long as you recognize what you are feeling and release the emotion from your mind and body, so that you can think clearly and choose to act in positive ways. The purpose of releasing emotion is to help you achieve inner peace.

Our culture also discourages crying, especially for men who are told almost from birth, "Big boys don't cry" or "Only sissies cry." But, as was discussed earlier, crying is an important way to release not just emotion, but physical toxins in our bodies. The idea of not only crying, but having a full-blown, two-year-old-style tantrum may seem absurd to some men, but I have found the tantrum exercise in this chapter to be one of the most liberating techniques for both men and women. Most people were discouraged from having tantrums when they were little and have a great deal of rage and sorrow to release. Even if you feel ridiculous at first, I hope you will try tantrum therapy.

The Inner Exploration Process is one of the most effective ways to release repressed emotions and their causes, but other methods are also used successfully by therapists to help people get in touch with their feelings. You can use the following therapeutic techniques on your own to become aware of your feelings and to release past and present emotions you may have suppressed safely. Experiment to find the ones that release your feelings at the deepest, most intense level. The more old emotions you release, the easier it will be for you to cope with distressing situations you encounter in the present.

Dealing with Anger and Frustration

If you repress or stuff your emotions, the emotions do not evaporate but are stored in your body until you release them. These stored emotions may later erupt in inappropriate situations or create stress that can result in disease. As a child, you may have been prevented from expressing your feelings and even punished for having had normal childhood tantrums. Those old feelings of rage and frustration may still be trapped inside you and can be triggered by present events, making our reactions more intense and painful than present circumstances warrant.

Tantrum therapy is an effective way to release feelings of anger and frustration. You simply allow yourself to have a tantrum—yes, a screaming, kicking, three-year-old tantrum. When you feel rage, frustration, or feelings of helplessness building inside you, lie face down on the bed, carpet, or something else soft so that you will not hurt your hands or feet. Begin beating with your fists, kicking your legs and screaming as loudly as you can. You will probably feel silly at first and you may even laugh. Keep going until strong feelings start coming out.

Scream anything you want. Sometimes yelling "No!" or "You can't do this to me!" or "Leave me alone!" or "Stop!" over and over will trigger your rage. Don't be afraid if your feelings are strong; that's why you stuffed them and why you need to get them out.

You may feel as though you'll lose control, but you won't. If you feel you might be overcome by your feelings, do multiplication tables in your mind to prove you have control. When you feel safe, let more of the rage out.

While you are having the tantrum, allow part of your mind to be a detached observer; notice what you are feeling in your mind and body. When did you feel this way as a child? Who are you really angry at? Tell that person how you feel and what you think of him or her.

Remember, you can't hurt anyone by expressing your feelings in private, but you *can* hurt others by stuffing your feelings until they burst out in an uncontrollable way.

Continue your tantrum until you feel a release of tension. When you reach and free your deep feelings, you will feel more relaxed and peaceful. After a few tantrums you may find that your anger has diminished to a point where you will not need this exercise anymore.

Controlling Emotions Quickly

If you are not in a place where you can have a tantrum, you can use this technique to quickly reduce intense emotional states so you can continue with your activities. This technique, called Cook's Hook-Up, is part of an innovative and effective program called Educational Kinesiology (Edu-K), which is being used successfully in therapy and in schools throughout the country to help children with learning disabilities.

People do not function well if the flow of energy in their bodies is obstructed or unbalanced. Strong emotions adversely affect the balance by increasing the energy above normal levels. Cook's Hook-Up is designed to balance the energy in your body so you feel more calm. Some people also use this technique to increase their energy level when it is low.

I know it sounds like nonsense, but it works! When you feel sad, angry, or afraid, sit comfortably in a chair or on a sofa, with your feet flat on the floor in front of you. Place your left leg on top of your right leg, so that your left ankle is on top of your right knee. Wrap your right hand around the top of your left ankle. Then grasp the toes of your left foot with your left hand. Yes, it's a bit of a contortion, but it's designed to make a complete circle of energy with your body.

Now place the tip of your tongue on the roof of your mouth, just behind your teeth. This is the position your tongue should be in when you inhale. Exhale through your mouth when it's slightly open, dropping your tongue back into the bottom of your mouth. So, you breathe in through your nose with the tip of your tongue at the roof of your mouth. Then drop your tongue to the bottom of your mouth and breathe out with your tongue relaxed and flat at the bottom of your mouth. Do this for thirty breaths.

Next, let go of your ankle and foot and put both feet flat on the floor. Your legs should be uncrossed for this part. Spread the fingers of your hands and touch the tips of each of your fingers together (thumb to thumb and pinkie to pinkie, etc.). Rest your hands in your lap with the fingers still spread and touching. Again breathe as you did before, inhaling with your mouth closed and the tip of your tongue at the top of your mouth, and exhaling with your mouth open and your tongue flat. Do this for another thirty breaths.

If you are really upset, you may need to do the two steps for a slightly longer time. As the energy balances, you may notice a slight tingling in your hands or feet.

Feeling Your Feelings

The best way to control emotions is not to control them. Often when people feel painful emotions they try to stop them, push them away, and deny that the emotions exist. Of course, there may be times when you do not want to explode in anger or burst into tears, such as when your are in a business meeting or with a child; at these times you do need to control your emotions. But if you can make time to be alone, the best way to understand and deal with your emotions is simply to feel them. The purpose of this exercise is to feel your emotions as intensely as you can, observe them, and allow them to flow through you.

Sit comfortably or lie down where you will not be disturbed. Take several deep breaths. People often stop breathing or breathe very shallowly when they feel strong emotions, and this automatic reaction seems to trap those emotions inside them. As you do this exercise remind yourself periodically to breathe deeply.

Close your eyes and permit yourself to really feel whatever emotion you are experiencing. This may seem scary at first because most of us do not allow ourselves to deeply feel our emotions. Strong emotions will not kill you if you release them, although they might cause harm in the long run if you repress them. You may be afraid that you will lose control, but I assure you that you won't. Keep breathing deeply.

Carefully observe how you feel in your mind and body. Where are there areas of tension, distress, or pain? What do those sensations remind you of—choking, stuffing feelings, nausea, being stabbed with a knife, burning? Describe to yourself mentally everything you feel as accurately as you can. Label your emotions and body sensations.

Now intensify your feelings. How strong can you make them? You can make them as strong as you want or turn them off. You are in control.

Breathe deeply and ask yourself when you felt this way as a child. Focus on your childhood memory as you feel your emotions even more intensely.

Continue to allow yourself to experience the emotion until the feeling shifts or diminishes significantly.

The more you do this exercise, the easier it will become and you will find that your emotional responses are less overwhelming and painful.

Integrating the Two Halves of Your Brain

This exercise from a method called Educational Kinesiology (Edu-K) helps to integrate the functions of both halves of your brain. The two hemispheres of the brain have different functions: The left is logical and handles thoughts, language, analysis, and the right side of the body; the right is emotional, and controls feelings, creativity, imagination, intuition, and the left side of the body. If you are to perform at an optimal level, the two hemispheres must be integrated, working together at the same time. But sometimes, usually due to traumatic experiences and intense emotions, one side of the brain will switch off.

If the emotional right side of your brain shuts down, you will react to situations without feeling. If the analytical left half switches off, your emotions will be exaggerated and out of control. This exercise helps restore a balance.

While standing, lift your left leg so that your foot is off the floor and your thigh is almost parallel with the floor; then slap the top of your left thigh with your right hand. Move forward as you step down on your left foot. Then do the same on the other side, lifting your right leg, thigh parallel with the floor, and slapping your right thigh with your left hand.

This part of the exercise is called *crossovers* because you keep alternating hands and legs as you prance around the room.

Continue with the steps and slapping. When you have mastered that part, look up to the ceiling on your left with your eyes only—without turning your head—and hum a note continuously. Do this for thirty or forty more steps.

Stop. Now raise your left hand and your left leg at the same time, like a puppet, and then repeat with your right hand and right leg. While you are stepping, look down to the right with your eyes only, without bending your head or shoulders. Do this for thirty or forty steps.

Now you are ready for integration. Slowly clasp your two hands together in front of you and feel the two halves of your brain working together.

Do the entire exercise twice a day for two weeks. If you have difficulty coordinating your hands with your legs during the crossovers, you need this exercise. Continue doing the crossovers until they are easy.

To test whether you have succeeded, sit down and close your eyes. With your fingernail, lightly draw an X in the middle of your forehead with each side of the X going down to an eye. You should be able to feel the X on your skin. Be sure to center the X in the middle of your forehead, just above your nose. Then with your eyes still closed, mentally picture where the X is. If the X stays in the center of your mental vision, your brain is integrated. If the X wanders to one side or the other, you need to continue doing this exercise.

After two weeks, evaluate whether your general emotional state has changed.

Empty Chair

This technique was created by Fitz Perl as part of Gestalt therapy, a psychological theory designed to increase self-awareness. The Gestalt therapist places an empty chair in front of the client and asks the client to imagine a parent or someone else sitting in the chair. The client is then directed to talk to that person as if he or she were actually there.

Another way of using the empty chair technique is to imagine that a part of yourself is sitting in the chair and to talk to that part. Then you switch sides, sitting in the formerly empty chair and responding to your own statements and questions. For example, if part of you is overly serious and does not have any fun, you can talk to that part and ask it why it prevents you from enjoying life. Then you switch chairs and answer, becoming the serious part of you.

You can also play different roles, switching chairs for each role. For instance, you might choose to be someone very strong and confident, and then switch to a helpless, "poor me" role. You can become aware of many subconscious thoughts and feelings by play acting various roles.

Using an empty chair to help you express your emotions can be particularly effective when you do not want to confront someone directly. The intent is to imagine as vividly as you can that the other person is actually present and to say everything you would really like to say to that person's face. But in this case there are no restrictions. You don't have to be polite or controlled or hold anything back. In fact, the purpose of the exercise is to release as much emotion as you can, so scream and swear if that will help you get your feelings out.

Start by telling the person what you feel, rather than what you think. Talk as though the person were present and call him or her by name. Explain what the person did to you and how much he or she hurt you. Be specific: "You hit me with a belt. You really hurt me—you bruised my back. You made me feel worthless and ashamed. I didn't deserve that. No one deserves that. Why did you do it? I loved you and you hurt me."

The most important part is to tell the person exactly how you felt about the act and about the person. Most people felt hatred at the time they were hurt but are terrified of admitting it. If you are afraid of expressing this hatred, force yourself to repeat, "I hate you!" screaming it if necessary, until the feelings start coming out. Continue to scream, "I hate you!" until all of the emotion has been exhausted. Sometimes it helps to also scream, "I wish you were dead!" or "I want to kill you!" Don't be afraid of these feelings; they are normal. They only become dangerous when they are suppressed. They can no longer control you when you acknowledge and release them. Once you release these feelings at a deep level, you will find an inner peace you never knew was possible.

Another ironic result is that once you release feelings of hatred and suppressed anger, it becomes easier to forgive the person. Repressed anger and hatred creates barriers between you and other people and can prevent you from feeling love. Only by releasing these feelings can you begin to feel closer to others, including the people who hurt you.

Physical Exercise—An Effective Antidote for Depression

Although clearing your past is the most effective and permanent cure for depression, regular exercise is also a powerful remedy and has immediate effects. It outperforms drugs, shock treatment, and psychotherapy. Exercise causes the brain to release endorphins, hormones that make you feel euphoric. These are the same hormones released during lovemaking. You may have heard of "runner's high," a state of bliss runners often experience that is somewhat like a drug high. Runner's high is caused by the release of endorphins, the same chemical that can be released through other less painful forms of exercise—providing the same euphoric effect.

Fast walking for thirty minutes to an hour a day, or at least every other day, is one of the best forms of exercise. It is low impact, does not damage your knees, and you don't need expensive equipment. Another advantage of walking is that it gets you outside so that you are exposed to sunshine. New studies indicate we need fifteen to twenty minutes outdoors in daylight every day (even if it's cloudy) to maintain a minimal level of physical health. An additional benefit is that you can watch other people (and perhaps meet and talk to them) and enjoy the antics of birds and other animals.

There are many forms of exercise, from stationary bicycles to dancing, skiing (my favorite), swimming, and team sports. Forget the "no pain, no gain" myth. Pick a form of exercise you enjoy. If you hate it, you won't keep it up.

If you are so depressed you can't get out of bed, you need professional help. Find a psychotherapist who can help you uncover the underlying reason for your depression, so that it will not recur. But you still need to get out and exercise. Put notes up around the house that remind you to force yourself to exercise. Ask a friend to come and drag you out of bed.

I strongly recommend that you exercise regularly while using the Inner Exploration Process because clearing your past can be stressful. You will find facing painful memories will be easier if you release stress through daily exercise. If you start exercising regularly, I guarantee you will feel better.

Healthier Breathing

You may think breathing is natural and that everyone automatically knows how to breathe properly. Not so. Many people breathe too shallowly and do not take in enough oxygen.

The way you breathe affects your mental state and your ability to deal with stress. When people are afraid, they momentarily stop breathing, and then breathe quickly and shallowly, usually moving their shoulders up and down. Children who are frequently frightened or under stress fall into the habit of breathing incorrectly, which, as adults, has negative effects on their moods and health.

Simply learning to breathe from your diaphragm can relieve depression and fear—and increase your energy.

Take a couple of normal breaths. If your shoulders are moving up and down, you are not breathing correctly. Your diaphragm, the area above your waistline just below your rib cage, should move outward when you inhale while your shoulders remain still.

Lie flat on your back on the floor and relax. You will automatically breathe correctly in this position and will be able to see your diaphragm rise and fall. Observe your diaphragm as you breathe, rising as you inhale and deflating as you exhale.

Concentrate on really filling your lungs, breathing as deeply and slowly as you can, feeling the air fill from the bottom of your diaphragm all the way up to your collarbone. Do this two or three more times and then relax and breathe naturally. This is how you should breathe all of the time.

Practice breathing while lying on the floor for a few minutes every day for a month. During the day, whenever you feel anxious or under stress, make a conscious effort to breathe from your diaphragm, taking slower, deeper breaths. As healthy breathing becomes a habit, you will feel noticeably better.

Deep Emotional Release: Conscious Connected Breathing

One of the most effective ways to release repressed emotions is a simple breathing technique known as conscious connected breathing, rebirthing, holotropic breath work, and other names created by various facilitators. Whatever the name, this method generally produces dramatic, immediate, and permanent healing effects.

I prefer the term *conscious connected breathing* because it describes the simple process. When people breathe normally, they tend to breath automatically, pausing between breaths, and often do not breathe deeply. In conscious connected breathing, breathing is the focus of our attention and becomes conscious rather than automatic. The person concentrates on breathing very deeply and one breath immediately follows another without a pause. This way of breathing brings more oxygen into the body, releasing suppressed emotions at a cellular level from the mind and body.

When people are under a great deal of stress, they stop breathing or breathe quickly and shallowly. This traps the energy of their emotions inside their bodies. Conscious connected breathing helps release the imprisoned emotional energy by overoxygenating cells and forcing the trapped energy out.

Psychiatrists in World War II found that soldiers who suffered from post-traumatic stress disorder were cured through the release of intense emotions. For this reason, many people have used conscious connected breathing as their primary technique for healing past trauma. When your old suppressed feelings are released, they disappear permanently, leaving you feeling noticeably lighter and happier, because the stored emotional energy is gone.

This technique has many surprising effects. It can release the stress that is causing physical symptoms and heal them. In fact, a deep emotional release can produce a dramatic alteration in posture, physical appearance, and health. Another amazing effect is that people who have had surgery using ether as the anesthesia may experience the smell of ether coming out of their bodies during breath work as their bodies release the poison of the ether and the trauma of surgery.

One of the extraordinary advantages of conscious connected breathing is its ability to reach emotions repressed in infancy and even in the womb. In this century, deep breathing techniques were developed by therapists who recognized that trauma during the birth process affected people throughout their lives. This breath technique was initially called "rebirthing" because it was used to release the repressed intense emotions and pain of being forced from the womb. Rebirthers found that their technique not only evoked emotions from trauma during birth, but those from childhood and adult trauma as well.

Even at the preverbal stage, children comprehend much more about what is happening than was previously thought. People using this breathing technique have been astonished to find themselves crying about not wanting to be born because during delivery they heard the doctor say they were too big and would hurt their mothers. Or they may have heard or felt that their parents did not want them. This technique is especially effective in releasing very early trauma, particularly preverbal experiences, because the emotions can be released without words.

People using conscious connected breathing may also have powerful spiritual experiences. According to psychiatrist Stanislav Grof and other breath work facilitators, many people experience nonordinary states of consciousness, including those similar to cosmic consciousness, during breath work. Some people use this technique for mind expansion, and some facilitators provide music especially composed to induce spiritual experiences by stimulating the chakras, the energy centers on the spinal column.

Conscious connected breathing is one of the most powerful and transformational techniques I have found and perhaps the most effective one for releasing deeply suppressed emotions, especially for people who have difficulty expressing or releasing their feelings. The only drawback is that it may not always uncover the damaging decisions you may have made or the lies you may have told about yourself. For that reason, I used a combination of conscious connected breathing and the Inner Exploration Process for clearing my mind.

Instructions for Conscious Connected Breathing

Conscious connected breathing can be tiring, so most people prefer to do this technique lying down on a sofa, massage table, or the floor. Lie on your back, with your arms and legs uncrossed and hands open. Shut your eyes and begin breathing deeply with your mouth open, emphasizing the inhalation and relaxing during exhalation. Breathe from you diaphragm, not your shoulders, and make your diaphragm rise as completely as you can, filling your lungs fully with each inhalation. The hard part is that, unlike normal breathing, you do not pause between breaths. As soon as you finish exhaling one breath, inhale another immediately.

For a while, nothing will happen. Just keep breathing deeply and consciously. It may take fifteen or twenty minutes for an emotion to arise. You cannot make an emotion come by willing it or forcing it to happen. You simply have to relax and keep doing the conscious breathing for as long as it takes. Whatever emotion you are ready to release will develop no matter what you are thinking, which is why conscious connected breathing is especially effective for people who think and analyze too much.

If you keep breathing deeply, slowly, and without a pause, you will begin to feel an emotion—and it will usually not be the one you expect. Sometimes you will feel a tingling sensation in your hands or feet, which means an emotion is starting to develop. Keep doing the breathing and allow the emotion to arise and intensify.

Once you feel the emotion intensely, it is important to continue breathing deeply and to allow yourself to feel the emotion fully, express it, and release it from your body. Keep your hands open and your arms and legs as straight as possible so the emotional energy can flow through you. If you close your hands, the energy may be trapped back inside you. When you become really emotional—screaming, sobbing, pounding pillows with rage—you can forget about how you are breathing. At that point, you need to express what you are feeling as freely and loudly as is helpful to you. This is not a time to hold back or maintain appearances. You need to scream, curse, roll on the floor, allow your body to jerk and release the pain—or whatever else you need to do to release your feelings.

People are often afraid that powerful emotions will make them lose control and hurt themselves or others. This does not happen. You will not lose control of your mind during this process, even if you experience emotions from memories of times when you felt you were going insane. Even while in the most intense emotional states, you will still be able to control your actions.

During the breath work process, I started feeling murderously angry at all the people who did not help me when I was being abused as a child, and ignored my bruises and pleas for help. As my emotions grew stronger, I realized I hated people and wanted to kill everyone. My breath work facilitator picked up a pillow, held it in front of him, and asked me to hit it. I was afraid of hurting him and I screamed at him to get as far away from me as possible. He said I would not hurt him, that no one had ever hurt him during breath work, but I pushed him away and pounded pillows on the floor instead. Despite the power of my feelings, I did not hurt him or myself, and once I released the hatred, I felt an incredible sense of peace.

Most of us have many layers of repressed emotion from years of buried hurts. Although you may sometimes feel that every last drop of emotion has been wrung out of you, there are usually deeper levels to uncover because we have all suffered a variety of profound psychological wounds.

You control how much emotion you release at each breath work session. If you want to decrease or stop the emotions, you simply stop the deep connected breathing. Just relax and slow your breathing down. Pause between breaths. The emotions will subside.

Sometimes even after you stop the conscious connected breathing, you may still feel the emotions, although with less intensity. This means feelings still need to come out. You may have to either go back to conscious connected breathing to release more of the feelings, or just release them physically by crying, screaming, or hitting pillows.

Warning: Sometimes conscious connected breathing can cause hyperventilation, which on occasion can lead to a condition where your body may freeze up and you cannot move. This can be frightening, especially if you are stuck in a strong emotion, but you can stop it by simply stopping the conscious connected breathing. Start breathing normally, relax, take breaths that are more shallow, and pause between each breath. Open the fingers of your hands because the energy can become trapped if your hands are clenched. You can handle this situation; it is not fatal or permanent.

Even after many breath work sessions when you believe you have released most of your suppressed emotions, you need to continue to release new emotions as they come up in order to remain clear. You can do this by dealing with your feelings as they arise, and by using conscious connected breathing to clear out stress as it builds up in your body. The advantage of connected breathing is that once you have learned the technique, you can use it whenever the need arises.

Conscious connected breathing releases the deepest, most intense layers of emotion from past experiences, often those emotions most hidden from your conscious mind, and allows them to be expressed in a safe way. While you are feeling the emotions, you will usually have thoughts and say things that will give you a sense of the events that caused the emotions. Some people recover clear memories of past events during breath work, but most only get a sense of what happened. For this reason, I found it helpful to use the Inner Exploration Process first to recover memories so I had a framework for what I experienced in breath work. Later I used conscious connected breathing to release the deepest layers of emotion that other therapies did not reach.

Working with a Facilitator or a Therapist

Although the technique is simple, most people prefer to have the support of a facilitator at first, to teach them how to sustain the breathing and support them through emotional release. The depth and intensity of feelings that arise can be frightening without the support of someone who can reassure you and help you continue breathing through your emotions. You do not need a facilitator or therapist, however, to use conscious connected breathing; many people do it by themselves. Sometimes people's emotions can be so violent and their body reactions so realistic, such as movements experienced during rape, that they prefer to do their work in private. I found that in most instances I could achieve deeper levels of emotion with the help of a facilitator.

Your support person does not have to be a licensed therapist, but does have to be someone you trust. The facilitator should also be familiar with the technique and have used it on him or herself so that he or she is comfortable with strong emotions and knows how they feel. The best facilitators are sensitive and compassionate, but the primary requirement for a breath work facilitator is that he or she has worked with the technique personally and is comfortable enough with strong emotions to help you through yours.

There is no need for a therapist because releasing the emotions is itself the therapy. No analysis is necessary. Most people recover enough memories or impressions of what happened to them during their emotional release to resolve the trauma without needing to have knowledge of the details. After you've used conscious connected breathing a few times and know how to evoke emotions and decrease them, you can start doing sessions without a facilitator.

However, as with other techniques in this book, conscious connected breathing can be used with a therapist or in conjunction with therapy. Breath work can also be done in groups where you work with a partner under the guidance of a facilitator. Whether you choose to work alone, individually with a facilitator, or in a group (where the fee is usually lower) is a matter of personal preference. One advantage of groups is that they are often held on weekends for several hours or even a day, so you have time to finish releasing whatever emotions you access that day. A disadvantage is that the facilitator may not be immediately available for another session if you need follow-up help. Sometimes the breath process can release emotions that continue to emerge for a few days following the session and you may want to have someone available for consultation. Before joining a group, find out if the facilitator will be available for emergencies and further work.

Breath work sessions usually last one-and-a-half to two hours, but a few of my sessions have lasted from three to five hours; group sessions in which participants act as facilitators for each other under the supervision of a leader may last for a day or weekend.

Conscious connected breathing seems to be the most effective technique for clearing out early emotional experiences. Breath work also avoids the Western tendency to intellectualize and rationalize feelings. With breath work, you cannot plan what will come out; whatever emotion is ready to be released will appear. This technique works regardless of intellectual capacity or language proficiency and it may be the most effective way for the mentally challenged, many of whom have been subjected to cruelty and humiliation, to release anguish and anger they may have repressed.

There are not enough psychotherapists today who know how to help people release repressed trauma. That is one reason why conscious connected breathing is such a valuable tool: It is a simple, natural way of healing at a deep and permanent level. Since this technique is free and people can do it by themselves, it is available to anyone who needs it.

Laughing

Laughter is a powerful antidote for depression. Some doctors believe laughter is the best medicine for healing. The purpose of this exercise is simply to find ways to laugh every day. Here are some suggestions:

- Watch funny television shows, movies, and videos. Norman Cousins watched old Laurel and Hardy and Charlie Chaplin comedies and laughed himself into curing his "incurable" disease.

- Read only newspaper comics for a week instead of the headlines and disaster stories and see how you feel.

- Observe children or animals playing. Join in and play with them.

- Play games with your family and friends that make you laugh. Have a party where you play games—word games, charades, children's games or board games—instead of standing around talking.

- Ask your family and friends to find amusing things to show or tell you and do the same for them. Limit your conversation to pleasant and humorous topics for a day—or a week. Observe how you feel.

- Tickle someone and let them tickle you back.

- Laugh at yourself.

Acts of Kindness

Helping someone is a surefire way to lift your spirits. The key to this exercise is not to expect gratitude. If you expect thanks, you may be disappointed. Simply do it for yourself, because you want to. Even if at first you are not sure you really want to, making the effort will be a rewarding experience.

Start by doing something simple, a small act of kindness for someone just because you know it will please them. Send a friend a card for no reason, to say you are thinking of them. Say hello or take a casserole to a neighbor. Mow someone's lawn, plant flowers, or shovel the snow off someone's driveway when they are out, so that they don't know who did it. Think of ways to make someone's life a little easier.

Do random acts of kindness for strangers. Give a meal to someone who is hungry. Visit someone who is ill or shut-in, and read him or her stories or poetry. Put coins in someone's parking meter because the time has expired. Send someone flowers without a card. Clean up the trash in your neighborhood or anywhere you think needs it.

If you want to feel really good, volunteer your services a couple of hours a week to help a child, an older person who may need company, or someone who is physically challenged. Join an organization that supports the arts or the enviroment. Choose something you would enjoy doing. The purpose is not to suffer or sacrifice. Volunteering is for you to get out, do something new, and meet new people.

9

Understanding Yourself

When you forgive, you take your enemy's power over you away, you defang them and change the atmosphere between you from highly charged to neutral, and sometimes even to rosy hued. And people, who had the power to control you just by being, can no longer command your emotions, or suck you into the vortex with a word. They cease to be the eye of your storm, and once you forgive them, they become people like any other, human and flawed and misguided on occasion, and hence rather like the rest of us.

—Merle Shain,
Hearts That We Broke Long Ago

You may think you know yourself, but most of us don't spend the time to really get to know what we think and feel—and why. These exercises are designed to give you new insights about yourself and fresh ways of looking at your problems. I find the drawing exercise particularly helpful because it works especially well for people who think too much— and it's fun. Drawing can reveal your true feelings, which are sometimes totally different from what you consciously believe.

The nursery rhyme and animal exercises may seem to be merely frivolous games at first glance, but it's amazing what they reveal about people's characters and their beliefs about themselves. As you do these exercises, keep in mind that you create your personality and can change any traits you want. Whatever you learn about yourself will give you greater awareness of who you are and will make more choices available to you.

Draw Your Problems

Many people are out of touch with their feelings, particularly men who have been taught to suppress their emotions almost from birth. Some can't describe their feelings; others feel nothing. People who are out of touch with their feelings generally are left-brain dominant: they operate primarily from the left-side of their brains, the side that is logical, factual, and analytical. This exercise helps people get in touch with their emotions through drawing, a right-brained activity that stimulates creativity and emotions.

You will need three or four pieces of plain paper (at least 8½ by 11 inches), a box of crayons or colored pens, and about an hour of uninterrupted time for this exercise.

Take a few deep breaths and relax. Then pretend you're a child and draw whatever you're feeling or a picture of a problem you're having. Draw quickly, without thinking too much about it. Scribble, doodle, or just fill the page with color.

Don't worry about making your drawing beautiful, accurate, or even representational. You are not being judged on your artistry, and neatness doesn't count. The object is to be free—experiment and play.

When you have finished, put your drawing aside. If you drew a feeling, draw a new picture showing yourself as a child when you may have felt the same way. If you drew a problem, draw a new picture of when you might have had a similar problem as a child or a picture of how it feels to have that problem.

When you finish your two drawings, look at the first one and label the feelings in it. Does it feel happy, sad, mad, scared, ashamed, or confused? If you have trouble describing the feelings, pretend someone else did the drawing. What do you think that person would be feeling if he or she did the drawing? Look at the dominant colors. Red can be happy in valentines, but in drawings of this type it usually indicates anger; we acknowledge the connection between color and emotions when we say someone who is really angry as "seeing red." We also refer to someone who is sad as "blue." Black generally connotes depression, hatred, and even death—a "black mood." Most of us tend to deny unpleasant emotions, so be aware of this tendency.

What do the colors in your drawing mean to you? If you find it difficult to describe your feelings in words, go through the short list of emotions in the paragraph above and ask yourself which ones fit the colors and subject matter in your drawing.

Do the same with your second drawing. Did making the second drawing help you better understand your feelings or problem?

It helps to do this exercise with a friend so that you can interpret each other's drawings. Someone else may often be able to see things in your drawing that you don't, especially if the feelings are painful. Be open to other ideas and consider those that are useful to you, but your own interpretations are the most valuable.

The last step is to change negative feelings and eliminate the problem by making another drawing. It is most effective to do all drawings the same day, but you can wait until the next day if necessary.

Psychologists have found that if we have a problem, being able to visualize or draw the problem as having been solved can actually help bring about that result. And sometimes drawing a happier picture can diminish painful emotions.

If you drew a painful feeling in the prior exercise, draw how you would feel if you were really happy. What would you and your world be like if everything were going exactly the way you want? What would you look like? How would you interact with others? As before, drawing skill is irrelevant here.

If you orginally drew a problem, now draw a picture of how you would feel if that problem were solved. You might draw how a relationship would look if it changed for the better or how you would act if you obtained something you desire. The object is to depict feelings of happiness and success.

When you finish this drawing, notice how you feel in your mind and your body. Is there any difference between what you feel now and how you felt when you started?

Whenever you begin to feel the old painful feelings, think of your new drawing; picture it in your mind and remember how you felt when you drew it.

Write to Your Inner Child

This exercise can be used when you are anxious, depressed, or angry and you are not sure why. You can also use it to uncover traumatic experiences in your past, release feelings about your parents and others, and understand the child part of you.

You will need a pad of paper, a pencil, a crayon, and about an hour of uninterrupted time.

Start by writing any thoughts you may have about your feelings or about a particular person or situation. Use the hand you normally use for writing. The object is to put down all of your uncensored thoughts and feelings as quickly as you can, without worrying about spelling or writing style.

Now pick up a crayon using your other hand, the one you don't normally use for writing. Ask the child part of you to express his or her thoughts and feelings, allowing yourself to write as freely as possible with the crayon. Write as large as you want and use as many pages as you need. Don't judge or censor what comes out. Just let as much emotion come out as you can.

When you think you have finished, ask your inner child if there is anything more. If you are sure there is nothing more, ask your inner child what he or she needs, what you can do to make your child feel better. Write the answer with the crayon.

Now use the adult part of your mind and read over what you have written. Mentally talk to your inner child, reassure him or her, and help your child correct any mistaken beliefs. Then give your inner child what he or she needs.

Awareness through Journaling

Writing daily in a journal or diary is a powerful way to learn more about yourself and to record your progress. Some people have a large journal next to their beds to record the day's events before they go to sleep. Others carry smaller journals with them and write their thoughts down as they occur. Choose the size and type of journal that works best for you. The most important thing is to get into the habit of writing in your journal on a daily or regular basis, so your recollections are fresh and detailed.

In order to increase your self-awareness, you need to record your thoughts and feelings about events; don't just describe what happened. What experiences make you happy, angry, sad, peaceful, confused, or anxious? Describe in as much detail as possible what led up to events that caused you distress. What did someone say? What were your thoughts about what was said? Your thoughts about events cause your emotional reactions, not the events themselves. How did you act on those feelings?

One of the chief benefits of keeping a journal is that you can express and release your feelings by writing about what you feel. Writing is a right-brained activity and emotions not only arise from the right side of our brains but are stored there as well. The physical act of writing about painful events provides a catharsis, a release of emotions, which will help you process and assimilate those events so you can put them to rest. By expressing your feelings as vividly as you can, you will let them out and prevent them from causing problems in the future.

Some people are almost totally unaware of their feelings. They have learned to suppress their emotions and may feel numb or dead. They do not know how to describe their emotional reactions. If asked how they feel, they will say something like: "I feel that _____ is trying to control me," or "I feel that you are angry." Anytime a sentence starts with "I feel that" or "I feel like," it is expressing a thought, not a feeling. An example of a true expression of feelings would be: "I feel angry (scared, confused, anxious) when I think _____ is trying to control me." Simply learning to distinguish between thoughts and feelings will bring greater awareness of your own reactions and will improve your communication and personal interactions.

Read over what you have written in your journal at the end of each week or at least the end of each month. When reading your journal, pretend it was written by someone else so you can view what you have written as an objective observer or therapist trying to learn as much as possible about the author. Your self-awareness will increase dramatically. You will begin to recognize patterns that repeat themselves in your relationships, emotional responses, and other experiences.

If you discover patterns you want to change, you may want to try the Inner Exploration Process and ask your mind to show you a memory or give you information that will explain the origins of this pattern and why you keep repeating it.

Some people use their journals as a way to become aware of what causes them stress. They keep a stress diary, a record of situations and personal interactions that make them feel tense or uncomfortable, with detailed descriptions of where they feel the tension in their bodies. This is helpful for becoming aware of your body's signals and what pushes your buttons, so you can learn to avoid stressful situations or deal with them more effectively. Make a record of every time you feel tense, restless, anxious, or annoyed. Describe how your body feels during the stressful incident: are your shoulders tight, are your fists clenched? Describe what thoughts are running through your mind at the time.

You will discover that different events and emotions cause specific sensations in different parts of your body. I get a pain under my right shoulder blade that means I feel anxious and think I'm not doing something well enough. A pain in the top of my shoulder means I'm pushing myself too hard. As I have become more aware of my body sensations,

I'm able to use the areas of stress to give me clues about what I'm feeling or thinking so I can change my thoughts and behavior—and react to events more effectively.

Many of us are not aware of what makes us happy and most of us tend to remember our failures rather than our successes. A valuable way to use a journal is to record all of your successes and moments of happiness. Describe the events in detail and record exactly how you felt, in your mind and your body. How did your head feel, your chest, your stomach, your legs? How did you walk and hold your body? Was your chin up or down? How did you talk? How did other people react to you? What did you feel about yourself?

You can use your success record in many ways, such as to cheer yourself up when you begin to focus on your failures and become depressed. Refer to your record of successes and moments of joy to remind yourself of who you really are and that the low times will pass.

Another way to use your success record is to learn from your experiences what makes you feel good and where you excel. Your success record will help you become aware of how it feels to be happy and successful. This awareness will enable you to recreate feelings of confidence and success in your mind and body more often, and you will be able to act more confidently simply by acting the way you did during your times of success. The way you feel about yourself determines how you react, act, and even move, and other people sense whether you feel like a victim or a hero. When you recall and recreate your feelings of success, you act differently, with more assurance, and you will be perceived differently. The results can seem miraculous.

Some people read over their success records to pump themselves up before job interviews and use examples from their records to impress employers.

Last, but certainly not least, many people have used their journals as a beginning for best-selling books. It is said that everyone has at least one good book in them, and, having heard hundreds of personal stories, I believe that is true. Each of us is special and has unique experiences and views of the world; we all have something to teach. Journaling may lead you into a new career in writing.

Your Favorite Nursery Rhyme or Fairy Tale

Fairy tales and nursery rhymes contain what psychiatrist Carl Jung called archetypal images. Our favorite rhymes and stories often reveal a great deal about our early lives and the psychological patterns established in our childhoods.

As a way of learning more about yourself, think about the stories and rhymes that affected you most. These may be the ones you liked the best, scared you the most, or simply the ones that come to mind. Choose one or two and then write down whatever you remember about them.

Now pretend you are a therapist and ask yourself how each story or rhyme applies to your life. What does it tell you about yourself and your childhood?

The rhyme I remembered the best was "Humpty Dumpty," and I always found it frightening. When I analyzed the words, I realized that I had felt torn into little pieces by the abuse in my childhood and felt that no one could put me back together. I wrote a new stanza to the poem about being able to put myself back together and several months later realized I had done it.

I also recalled the more positive story, *The Little Engine That Could.* Although I did not always remember that story consciously, I know that subconsciously it gave me the strength to go on.

If you discover something distressing in your favorite rhyme or story, write a new ending to the story or a new stanza to the rhyme, changing it to the way you would like it to be. Sometimes rewriting the ending can resolve a long-standing conflict in your mind.

What Animal Would You Like to Be?

You can learn a lot by observing animals. Here's a revealing exercise that can also be used at parties to get to know people: Choose an animal that you would like to be. Then write out why you have chosen that animal. What characteristics or abilities does that animal have that you would like to have?

Think about all of your animal's qualities. Which ones apply to you now?

What do you need to do to have the other qualities you want?

Mime Exercise

Your facial expressions reflect how you feel, but your expressions also affect your feelings. If you are feeling sad, smiling can actually make you feel better. Yes, even forcing a smile! If you don't believe this, try this exercise, which comes from the art of mime.

Make a very sad face in your mirror and hold it for a minute or so while you observe how a sad expression makes you feel. Notice how you feel in your mind and your body.

Now make an angry face and see how that feels.

Do the same for fear.

Then make a happy face.

Do you feel different?

Understanding Your Parents

As children, we think our parents are all-powerful. They seem to know our very thoughts. Because we are tiny, they seem supernaturally large. Because they are older, they seem to have infinite knowledge.

As children, we do not realize that our parents have problems of their own. And since most parents hide their fears from their children, we think our parents are confident and unafraid—that they have everything under control. As children our very survival depends on our parents, so we have to see our parents as infallible because if they are not, then there is no security in our world.

The sad fact is that even when we become adults, we tend to see our parents as we did when we were children, and react to our parents as if we were still children. This exercise is designed to help you break out of your childhood patterns.

Sit quietly, close your eyes and picture one of your parents in your mind. Visualize that parent with as much detail as you can. See that parent in different situations, with a spouse or partner, with friends, at work, and so on.

Now ask yourself whether that parent has it all together. Is that parent a well-adjusted, happy, secure person? Does that parent have all the answers? Does that parent always tell the truth?

The next step is to mentally picture that parent when you were a child, when your parent was younger. Recall as vividly as you can a time when that parent hurt you. See in your mind as clearly as possible how that parent looked when he or she was hurting you.

Now ask your adult self, was that parent a well-adjusted, happy, secure person? What might that parent have been feeling? Did that parent have all the answers? Did that parent tell the truth or know what the truth was? Do you always act the way you would like to act with your children or friends? Are your expectations of your parents reasonable?

Often we expect our parents to give us love that they simply are not capable of giving. We keep trying to get the love we needed as children, demanding that our parents change and act towards us the way we want them to act. The hard truth is that we cannot change our parents or make them change. They have to change themselves and may never do so. It is important to develop healthy boundaries so that you do not allow your parents to continue to hurt you. (You might try the exercise on page 163, Establishing Healthy Boundries.)

You can choose to avoid your parents or to accept them as they are and not expect them to change or love you in the way you want. Unless your parents still act abusively toward you, the latter is the healthier choice. Whether or not you choose to have a relationship with your parents, you need to forgive them by letting go of your angry feelings. Forgiving does not mean condoning what was done or forgetting it. It simply means letting go of your own anger so the people who hurt you no longer have power over you. Until you let go of your anger, you will find the same problems in eveyone you try to love.

How You Select Your Reality

What we focus on creates out perception of reality. We are literally unable to see some things while we are focused on others. A coin has a head and a tail, but if you are looking at one, you cannot see the other— even though they are part of the same whole.

The phenomenon of selective perception is the premise of an ancient teaching about three blind men who use their hands to find what an elephant is. The first man says the elephant is a cord with a tuft of hair on the end, a tail. The second says, "No, it's not like that at all. It's a huge ear." The last says, "You're both wrong; it's a long curvy thing that throws water." Each man experiences only part of the total picture, the part on which he focused.

When you are totally absorbed in listening to music, you will not be consious of seeing the details of objects around you. If you are concentrating on reading a fascinating book, you may not hear noises around you, or even someone calling your name, until you stop reading and focus on the sounds.

To experience selective perception, hold your hand about six to eight inches from your face and focus your eyes on your hand. Then focus your eyes on the wall beyond your hand. Now try to focus clearly on both your hand and the wall at the same time. It's impossible. When you are focusing on one, you cannot see the other clearly.

This is similar to what happens when we see the world through the filter of our beliefs. If we believe the world is violent and cruel, we will see examples of violence and cruelty all around us, and ignore acts of kindness. If we believe the world is kind and loving, we will see examples of kindness and love.

To experience this phenomenon, choose a day to consciously focus only on acts of kindness. In the morning, before you get out of bed, make a mental resolution to search for acts of kindness throughout the day. Keep a pad of paper and pen with you, and record each kind act you observe.

If you see unkind acts or have negative thoughts, such as, "There are no acts of kindness," or "I'll never be able to do this," simply acknowledge that it's okay to have those thoughts and affirm to yourself that you will focus on acts of kindness. Then look around carefully for another act of kindness. You don't have to believe that you will see acts of kindness, simply saying in your mind or out loud that you intend to do so is sufficient.

Record *all* kind acts: people being polite and respectful to each other, thanking each other, showing concern for each other, doing their jobs with care. Kindness is not limited to dramatic acts of heroism, although these are included. Write with as much detail as possible whatever kindness you observe.

Before you go to sleep, read over what you have written and think about how you feel about yourself, other people, and the world. Did you experience enough positive results from this exercise to do it for another day?

10

Nurturing Yourself

Of all the people there are in your lifetime, you are the only one you will never lose and the only one who will never leave.

—John Bradshaw

Caring for yourself now is just as important as clearing the past. As adults, we often feel lonely, unloved, and unlovable. We seem to have an insatiable need for love and approval, but no matter how many compliments we receive or how many successes we have, we feel empty inside. Deep down, many of us believe our needs will never be met and so we see our lives as perennially unfulfilled. These feelings are not unrealistic; they are based on facts that were once painfully true. We felt alone when we were children; no one met our needs for safety, love, comfort, security, affection, caring, kindness, dependability, and nurturing. The more deprivation we experienced, the greater our adult need to make up for what we lacked as children.

Adults who have been deprived of nurturing as children are like cups without a bottom. No matter how much love and approval goes in, it is never enough to fill the cup. The bottom of the cup, the foundation for an adult's sense of love and security, is established early in childhood through consistent love and nurturing bestowed on a child by his or her parents. But this does *not* mean that if you were deprived of nurturing as a child, it is lost to you forever. You can create your own foundation and repair the bottom of your cup.

This process is known as nurturing, or reparenting, yourself. You have the ability to give yourself the love and nurturing you did not receive as a child. You can become the loving parent you did not have. Although you cannot change what happened to you as a child, you can give yourself what you lacked. You can fulfill your own needs.

The most important step in nurturing yourself is learning to love the child in you. Most of us cannot bear to acknowledge the pain we felt in childhood, and many of us blocked it out of our conscious minds. Many of us never really had a chance to be children. We were forced to cope with events and emotions far beyond our years and did not experience freedom or fun.

I was no exception. As an adult, I was an intense, serious overachiever. During therapy, I poured over my childhood photographs for clues as to what I was like as a child. Since my father was a camera buff, there were hundreds of photos to choose from. But I could find none of a smiling, happy child—only a sad looking girl with shell-shocked eyes.

I cannot remember ever running and shouting with joy. I rarely played games, unless forced by my teachers. I never acted like a child; I was too busy just trying to survive.

This may sound all too familiar to you. If you look at your own childhood photographs, you will see how sensitive and vulnerable you were. Looking at childhood photographs can reveal a great deal about how you felt and what your life was like. It may be painful for you to see the hurt child you were, but you will begin to know yourself.

Many people deny their child parts because of the hurt they still carry inside. They do not want to have to admit how helpless and terrified they used to be, and still are inside. Some people hate who they were as children because they felt weak and vulnerable. But that child is still inside you, and the sad fact is that as long as you hate a part of you, you cannot love yourself and you are not able to accept love or love others.

If you want to heal the child (or child parts) in you, you must get to know that child. Search your memories for information about what you were like as a child. Did you change at some point? Did you lose your innocence, your joy, your affection, your spontaneity? What decisions did you make about yourself, about others, and about your life? What made you change?

After I uncovered memories of my childhood abuse and saw what I had survived, I began to have enormous admiration, even awe, for myself as a child. As I learned more about that child and how I coped, I began to realize my strengths and abilities, and the incredible power of my mind.

But starting to appreciate the child in me was not enough. I still had to learn to nurture that child in order to feel fulfilled as an adult.

There are many ways to nurture yourself and these exercises will help you begin. The guiding principle is to take good care of yourself and treat yourself with mercy, loving-kindness, forgiveness, compassion, and respect.

Reparenting Your Inner Child

One of the most effective ways to nurture yourself is to give the child inside you gifts you wanted as a child. Buy yourself a baby blanket, teddy bear, electric train, or doll—the toy you wanted most. Whatever you buy should be just for you—and it should be the best. No discount stores. You want to show your child that he or she is special, worth the best—and that *you* can provide it.

If you cannot afford to buy a gift, make a gift or special meal for your child, or take your child on a walk in a beautiful place and help him or her appreciate the beauty. One of the best things you can do to nurture your child is to get to know him or her and really listen to the child's experiences and feelings. Take the time to find out what your inner child needs—what *you* need. The point of this exercise is to show your child that you really care about him or her—and yourself.

The idea is to spoil yourself, lavish yourself with the love you lacked. Many people deny themselves the love and attention they need, although they may be very good at taking care of others. you must learn to love yourself and not compound your childhood deprivation by skimping on yourself emotionally or financially. Know that you are deserving of love and abundance. Allow yourself to give your inner child the kind of love you've always wanted, deep down. You cannot give a child too much love, especially one as hurt as you.

Learn to play and have fun. Take your inner child to places you always wanted to go, such as Disneyland, a baseball game, or the zoo. Act the way you would have liked to act as a child. Teach your inner child to swim or ski. See how high you can swing at a playground. If you feel silly playing by yourself, take your own kids or someone else's, but do what *they* want to do, let them lead and be one of them.

Be nice to yourself. Take time for yourself. Improve your mind, your health, and your life. Take a class or workshop. Get a massage. Exercising and taking care of your body is another way of nurturing yourself. By taking care of yourself, you are demonstrating that you value yourself and are worth the effort.

Find new things you enjoy doing for relaxation. When you give yourself pleasure, you are affirming that you like yourself and deserve to be happy. You are also proving that you can make yourself happy; you are not dependent on anyone else.

No one will ever be able to take care of you the way you want—except you. So pamper yourself and treat yourself as the special person you are. Take a bubble bath, read poetry, listen to music, go to bed early, take a nap. Send yourself flowers; especially if you are a man. Do something each day that makes you feel good.

And don't forget to thank yourself.

Visualizing Your Own Special Place

You can nurture yourself through a visualization exercise where you meet your inner child. Close your eyes and use the progressive muscle relaxation exercise on page 149. When you are relaxed, visualize yourself in a beautiful place, your special place, a place where you feel safe and at peace. It might be a beautiful garden, the seashore, a meadow, the mountains, a park, a garden, or even Disneyland. This is your special place, so make it just right for you. If my words do not fit, ignore them, and make your place and your experience just the way you want it to be, a place of total peace and beauty. If you find it difficult to relax and feel safe, you might build walls or fortifications around you or call upon whatever animals or people you need to protect you and help you feel safe.

Picture yourself in your special place. The sun is shining and you can feel its warmth on your head and shoulders. The sky is a beautiful, brilliant blue, and perhaps some soft white clouds float by. You can feel the warm, gentle gold rays of the sun on your head and shoulders; you are surrounded by a gentle golden light. You may feel a cool breeze caressing your skin.

Perhaps you smell the scent of the sea, flowers, or pine trees. You may hear the pounding of waves, a trickling brook, or bird calls. Perhaps you can see small birds soaring overhead or furry animals coming out to be fed. This is your special place and you can make it exactly the way you want it to be. You can come to this place in your mind whenever you want.

Picture yourself walking around, enjoying the beauty of your special place. After you have explored a while, you see someone walking toward you. It is a young child. As this child approaches, you see that it is you as a child. The child is so happy to see you, and runs toward you to give you a hug. Talk to the child and get to know him or her. Show the child around your special place and play with him or her; walk together hand in hand or just sit quietly together.

Then give the child a gift you know he or she needs, a special gift that will help him or her, one you know the child wants more than anything else. This gift can be tangible, such as a special toy or clothing, or intangible, such as love or approval.Your gift makes the child very happy and the child thanks you. You may continue to talk to your child or come out of your state of relaxation.

You might want to record this visualization so that you can play it to yourself while you are in a state of relaxation. Speak slowly and softly and pause after some of the paragraphs so you have time to enjoy your special place and the events in your mind.

Some people may feel angry at their child because they feel the child was weak and vulnerable. If you feel this way, do your best to find out more about the child, what the child experienced, and what he or she did so you could survive.

You can use this visualization as often as you want to learn more about yourself as a child and to give yourself love.

Another powerful way to send love to the child in you is to talk to that child in your mind and visualize hugging and kissing him or her goodnight. Imagine yourself as an adult taking care of the child the way you wish someone had taken care of you. Hold your child and let him or her cry; or cuddle, soothe, and show the child that he or she is safe now.

One of my clients who had been brutally abused as a child visualized hugging, kissing, and comforting herself at different ages every night, and sometimes during the day, for several weeks. When the child parts of her learned to feel comfortable accepting love, this woman began to like herself as an adult for the first time in her life. This technique works wonders; you will find that when you become comfortable loving yourself as a child and your child accepts that love, you will love yourself as an adult and you will see an abundance of love in the world around you.

Nurturing Affirmations

Using affirmations to reprogram negative thoughts can be a potent way to nurture yourself. Affirmations are positive statements you say or write to yourself as a way of consciously challenging self-defeating ideas. Simply affirming a positive thought to yourself invokes the power of your subconscious mind to make that thought come true. Your subconscious is like a giant computer, accepting what you tell it without analyzing or judging what you put in. You can program your subconscious mind to think negatively or positively and your subconscious will follow the instructions of your conscious mind and make them a reality.

For the best results, repeat each of your affirmations at least three times, two or three times a day. Yes, the magic formula in fairy tales has some validity; three is the minimum number for your mind to accept an idea at the deepest level, the subconscious. The more you repeat affirmations, the more effective they are. The best times to say your affirmations are in the morning before you get out of bed and at night before you fall asleep, because you are relaxed and your mind is in a receptive state. Louise Hay, the best-selling author of *You Can Heal Your Life,* suggests saying "I approve of myself" three or four hundred times a day for a month to overcome all of the negative things we have said to ourselves throughout our lives.

Affirmations should always be positive statements. If you say "I am not stupid," your subconscious mind only hears the word "stupid." Substitute "I am intelligent" or "I learn quickly," Keep your affirmations short because you have to say them many times.

Of course your affirmations must be realistic. If you are a four-foot-tall adult, you will not become six feet tall no matter how many times you repeat an affirmation. The most effective affirmations are the ones you use to nuture yourself and to counteract negative thoughts. The truth is that you are lovable and valuable. The best affirmations are the ones that help you believe the truth. Most people are so critical of themselves. Repeating affirmations helps you get into the habit of talking nicely to yourself—and to become your own best friend.

An important part of nurturing and reparenting yourself is convincing yourself that you can fulfill your needs. If your needs were not fulfilled when you were a child, you may believe they will never be fulfilled, and you will have a strong tendency to draw circumstances to yourself that confirm your belief. For example, if you believe no one will ever love you, you will constantly test your friends and lovers, watching for any slight or betrayal. And what you expect, you will find.

The truth is that your needs for love, acceptance, and approval cannot be fulfilled by others. You are the only one who can fulfill those needs. Using affirmations, you can reprogram your mind to override the old beliefs that keep you from having what you want.

State positively to yourself several times each day, especially in the morning before you get up and the evening before you go to sleep: "I fulfill my needs. My needs are fulfilled. I am a good person. I am lovable." If you do not feel ready for such direct statements, you might say, "I choose to fulfill my needs," "I can fulfill my needs," or "I choose to be lovable." You do not need to consciously believe your words; repeatedly saying and thinking them will reprogram your mind at a subconscious level. As you become more comfortable with these affirmations, you will find your conscious belief increasing.

However, there may be instances where a negative belief is so strongly imprinted in your mind that repeating affirmations is not enough to erase them. In such cases, the Inner Exploration Process is the most effective remedy for deleting the belief at the deepest level of your subconscious.

A writing technique using your affirmation can also be helpful. If your mind is resisting an affirmation, make a vertical line down the middle of a piece of paper, dividing it into two equal halves. On the left side of the page, starting at the top, write your affirmation over and over. For example, you might start writing, "I am lovable." Notice what thoughts come into your mind as you continue to write this affirmation. Whenever you have a negative thought, write it on the right side of the page. If you think, "No, I'm bad," or "But if I was lovable, my mother would have loved me," write those thoughts on the right side. Then go back to writing your affirmation over and over down the left side. Continue this process until you can write your affirmation at least a dozen times without having any negative thoughts—and without hesitation.

Sometimes if people feel unworthy or believe their needs will not be fulfilled, they unconsciously push love and success away. Repeating, "I accept love, support, and approval from all those around me," while working through feelings of unworthiness, can change this pattern.

Open your arms in a wide embrace and shout: "I accept all good. I accept love and abundance." The words and gesture declare to the universe that you are ready to accept love, prosperity, and abundance. Do this until you can shout the words without embarrassment or doubt.

Get Your Daily Quota of Hugs

Studies show that we need touch as much as we need food and water. We actually *need* to be hugged several times daily in order to maintain our health; some studies say at least four hugs a day, others twelve.

Look for people to hug and fill your daily quota. Hug your loved ones lots—for no reason. Hug your pet, unless it's a goldfish. there may even be colleagues at work you would feel comfortable hugging—but ask if they would feel comfortable first. Hug a tree and feel its strength; it really is a remarkable experience.

Ask for hugs, especially if you are feeling low or think you don't deserve them. Just say, "I really need a hug," and watch what happens. You will find that most people love to give hugs— they just need a little encouragement.

Greet your friends with a hug. Congratulate people with a hug. Thank them with a hug. Say goodbye with a hug.

Hug yourself.

Feel Happier Quickly

Whistle or sing. Dale Carnegie, the millionaire philanthropist, said you cannot feel unhappy while singing or whistling and recent neurobiological studies confirm that these acts have positive effects physically as well as mentally.

List fifty things you like, or list fifty things for which you are grateful.

Learning from Experience

Power and growth come from painful experiences, and most people have suffered in various ways. You may believe that your life would be better if you had not had these experiences, and consequently you may overlook the valuable lessons you learned from them.

This exercise is to make a list of all of the positive things you learned from the worst experiences of your life.

At first you may think that nothing positive could possibly come from these events. Take some quiet time to think of helpful things you learned about yourself, other people, survival, and life in general.

Would you be willing to give up what you gained?

Rewarding Yourself

You may often wait for people to notice the nice things you do and to compliment or reward you. And you may be disappointed when they don't. But part of growing up is learning to reward yourself.

Think about nice things you have done or things you have done well. Praise yourself and reward yourself for these things—and for trying so hard—by doing something special for yourself. Take time for yourself or buy yourself a gift you have always wanted. Thank yourself often.

Caring for Yourself

Sit quietly, take some deep breaths, and use your favorite technique to become relaxed. Remember or imagine a time as a child when you felt really cared for, when you felt safe because someone you cared for and trusted was there. Picture in your mind how it felt to have that caring person with you. Sense how that feeling of safety felt in your mind and in your body.

Picture in detail the caring concern that this person gave to you. Hear the tone of this person's voice. What did this person say? Were you addressed with respect? What did this person do? How did this person look? How did you feel in your mind and how did your body feel? What did you think about yourself, the caring person, and your world? Bring this picture towards you, closer and closer, until you know that it is your reality.

Now see yourself taking the place of the caring person. Feel yourself in that person's place. Notice how much you love this wonderful child. See the strength and intelligence of this little child, this unique being. Feel your connection to this special, loving little person.

Do you want to reassure this child? Think about what you could do to reassure the child and make him or her happy. Tell the child of your love.

And while you hold a picture of the capable, resourceful adult-you, once again mentally step into the child. Accept this offering of love from the capable adult-you. See the adult-you there, always available to help and protect you. Memorize what it feels like to be safe and protected. Thank this part of you for always being there to help and protect you.

Continue to feel a connection with your adult and child selves. When you know that you are fully connected to an adult that can handle any situation and you feel safe, open your eyes.

Getting the Help You Want

Taking care of yourself does not mean doing it all alone. Many people are reluctant to ask for help, no matter how much they need it. They may think requesting help shows weakness or makes them vulnerable.

If you were hurt as a child or your needs were ignored by your parents or caretakers, you may have difficulty trusting others. You may have made a conscious or unconscious decision that you cannot depend on anyone, that the only person you can rely on is yourself.

While growing up means taking responsibility for your actions and reactions, it does not mean that you have to do everything for yourself. Human beings are social animals. There are billions of us on this planet so that we can help each other. People who say that you have to "pull yourself up by your own bootstraps" apparently have never considered how ridiculous that idea is. Picture yourself trying to pull yourself up by straps on your shoes. It's impossible. You'll stay on the ground. But two strong friends can lift you up easily.

You are not being a burden when you ask people for help. If they don't want to help, they can always say no. Most people like to be asked for help; it makes them feel useful and important. Isn't that the way you feel when someone asks for your help or advice?

Instead of keeping your problems to yourself fearing that no one will understand, talk to a friend. You will find that your problems are not unique. People you don't know well may seem to have "perfect" lives, but inside most have a great deal of pain and feel unworthy. Often we can help each other even when we cannot help ourselves. The more open you are about your problems, the more your friends will confide in you, and the closer and more rewarding your relationships will become. This is especially true for men who are only beginning to share their experiences and seek support.

Make a resolution that you will ask someone for help at least once a week, or once a day if you can. Ask family members for help with chores, join a support group, or ask the advice of a colleague at work. Doing unpleasant tasks can be more fun with a friend and you can return the favor and spend more time together. Don't assume that people "know" you need help. If you want help, you need to ask for it directly. Of course you need to use some discretion in choosing who you ask; avoid people who are manipulative or who have hurt you in the past. Most people will respond warmly to requests for help, but if some don't, do your best not to take it personally; they have their own problems. Ask someone else.

Learning to Love Yourself

Most people never really see themselves. Even though they look in a mirror while dressing, they usually only see the teeth they are brushing, the hair they are combing, or the beard they are shaving. This exercise involves really looking at and accepting yourself, all of you, even the parts you may think you don't like.

Take some time each day to look in a mirror and closely observe your face and body. If there is a part of you that displeases you, ask yourself what that part does for you and what you would be like without that part.

Now look directly into your own eyes for a few seconds. What do you see?

While still looking into your eyes, tell yourself out loud, "I love you!" If you find it difficult to say this sincerely and enthusiastically, you need to do this exercise.

Continue to say, "I love you!" when you look at yourself in the mirror every day until you can say it comfortably and lovingly, without flinching or looking away.

11

Changing Old Thought and Behavior Patterns

Life consists in what a man is thinking all day.

—Ralph Waldo Emerson

The techniques in this chapter are designed to help you increase your awareness of negative thoughts and behaviors and break old habits. Although the Inner Exploration Process is the most effective technique for changing unwanted thought and behavior patterns at the deepest level, sometimes it is helpful to use a variety of techniques to attack a problem. My two favorite exercises in this chapter are the ones based on ancient Zen meditations, Facing Your Worst Fear and What Would Happen If You Got What You Wanted Most? These exercises address core issues and the results can be powerful and surprising. I deliberately avoided describing what might happen when you do these exercises because the results are highly individual and I do not want to spoil your experience by giving you specific expectations. As with all of the exercises in this book, whatever you get from them is exactly what you need.

However, it is important to take sufficient time to do these exercises thoroughly; don't rush through them. You may also have potent new insights if you repeat these exercises several weeks or months later.

Although several of my psychotherapy clients benefited from the self-defeating thoughts exercise, I personally had little success with it. However, therapists have used this exercise for decades and many people have benefitted from it. Try everything until you find something that works for you.

Facing Your Worst Fear

This exercise is based on a Zen meditation and can help you overcome your deepest fears.

Sit quietly in a chair with your arms and legs uncrossed and your spine straight. Close your eyes and take a few deep breaths, feeling the air flowing in and out of your lungs.

When you feel calm, think about your worst fear. What is the worst thing that could possibly happen to you? Is it having cancer, experiencing the death of a loved one, losing all of your possessions, being alone?

When you have identified your worst fear, imagine this fear coming true. Visualize it in your mind in as much detail as possible using all of your senses. What would you see around you? What sounds would you make or hear? What would you smell? How would it feel in your mind and body for this fear to be true?

You may start feeling some strong emotions. Don't stop them from coming out. You need to feel these emotions and see that they cannot destroy you. Instead of fighting your emotions, let them flow through you. Intensify them, if you can. Magnify them and see how these strong emotions feel in your mind and throughout your body. Become an observer of your feelings.

Envision all of the consequences of your worst fear coming true. What would happen and how would you feel the first day? Visualize the first day in detail. What would you do, who would you talk to, how would you act?

When you have exhausted everything you can imagine happening during the first day, go on to the second day and visualize that day in detail; focus on what you would feel and what you would do. Visualize several successive days in detail and then skip to the next week, then the next month, and then the next year. What would your life be like as time passes? How would you feel in your mind and body? What would you do on a day-to-day basis? How would you interact with people? What changes would you make in your life? Keep going until your feelings shift or dissipate.

Meditate on what you have learned.

What Would Happen If You Got What You Wanted Most?

This is a companion Zen exercise to the preceding one. It is especially effective for workaholics and people driven to succeed, as well as those who believe they must have a certain partner, job, or other material thing to be happy. This exercise consists of imagining what your life would be like if you got whatever you want most.

Eastern religions advise against attachment to worldly desires. An ancient Chinese proverb warns: Be careful what you ask for; you might get it! The idea of attachment is often misunderstood by Westerners who think it means not to want anything or not to love or care about anything or anyone. In fact Eastern religions encourage people to enjoy the wonders of the planet, but not to the extent of wanting something so desperately that they believe their happiness depends on having it. People are frequently unhappy because they do not have what they think they want. You may be afraid of losing something or someone, or you may be putting off happiness, saying to yourself that you will be happy when you graduate, have enough money, find the perfect partner, and so on. Most people spend far too much time worrying about getting what they think they want— what they believe they can't live without.

Sit quietly and take some deep breaths. Focus on your breathing as you inhale and exhale deeply and slowly. Feel your breath entering your nostrils, filling your lungs, and then leaving your lungs through your nostrils. In and out. In and out.

When you feel relaxed, think about what you want most, what you believe you need in order to be happy. Then imagine that you have whatever you believe would make you happy.

Picture what it would be like to have exactly what you want. Imagine the situation in as much detail as possible. How would you feel in your mind and body? What would you say? How would you look? How would you walk? What would your relationships be like? Would your life change? What would your life be like?

Imagine the first day, visualizing in detail what your life would be like moment by moment when you have what you want. Use all of your senses; imagine how you would feel, what you would see, what you would wear, how you would act, how people would react to you, what they would say to you, and what you would do during the day.

When you have gone through the first day in detail from morning to night, do the same for the next day, and then the next until you have vividly pictured how your life would be for a week.

Then imagine in detail what your life would be like the next month and the one after that. What would your life be like in a year? How would you feel? Picture in detail a day in your life a year later and then a year after that. Would your life be different? In what ways? How would you feel about your life and yourself?

Spend a few minutes thinking about what you learned from this exercise.

Stopping Self-Defeating Thoughts

Most of us have a constant stream of self-criticism running through our minds and are harder on ourselves than on anyone else. If you were in a restaurant and overheard people at the next table talking to each other the way you may talk to yourself, you would probably be horrified. The flow of self-put-downs can seem unending: "You're stupid"; "You can't do anything right"; "No one could ever love you"; "You did it wrong again—you'll never learn"; "You're lazy."

Although some people are unaware of their negative self-talk the results can still be disastrous. These put-downs destroy self-esteem and trap people in self-defeating patterns of behavior that can ruin their lives. As I explained in chapter 1, your thoughts send directions to your subconscious mind, which in turn controls your body and the way you perceive the world. Each time you put yourself down, you direct your mind and body to make you act in a way that confirms the negative statement. So each time you tell yourself you're stupid, you are directing your subconscious mind to make you act that way and confirm your belief.

Although I believe the Inner Exploration Process is the most effective way of eliminating destructive beliefs about ourselves, another method is to become consciously aware of your negative thoughts and develop the habit of stopping them. This is a technique called *thought stopping,* a cognitive therapeutic technique used by many therapists that does not involve uncovering memories or emotions.

The process is simple, although its implementation can be challenging. The first step is to become aware of what you say to yourself in your mind. It helps to keep a written record of all the negative things you say to yourself during a day or a week. Write everything down, whether it is large or small. You will begin to see a pattern emerge.

The next step is to stop these thoughts whenever you become aware of them. If you find yourself thinking "I'm stupid," immediately say to yourself in your mind, "Stop!" Some people find it helpful to see the word "Stop!" in their minds in large red letters. Others hear themselves shouting the word in their minds. Author Louise Hay uses a gentle but firm, "Thank you for sharing," to cut off further criticism. Use whatever technique works best for you.

After you have recognized the negative thought and stopped it, the last step is to immediately change each put-down to a positive statement, an affirmation, and repeat it in your mind. For example, if one of your thoughts was that you are stupid, you might change the thought to "I'm intelligent," or "So I made a mistake—it's okay to make mistakes, everyone does, and I'll learn from it." Don't use negatives such as "I'm not stupid," because your subconscious mind hears only the operative words like "stupid" and may ignore the negative. Use short, positive statements and repeat them as many times in your mind and out loud as is convenient. The more you say the positive statements, the more your subconscious mind will accept the idea. You need to say the positive statements many times to counteract all the times you have put yourself down.

The same technique can be used for obsessive thoughts and scary thoughts about disasters, wanting to kill someone, or any other distressing thought that you want to eliminate. If you see awful pictures or situations in your mind, change them to pleasant ones, with happy outcomes. If the distressing thoughts persist, use the Inner Exploration Process to uncover the cause or see a professional for support.

Your thoughts are not you. You have control over your mind and can stop your thoughts, whatever they are. Sometimes it seems difficult to imagine pleasant situations in place of old thoughts and experiences, but the results are worth the effort.

The purpose of this exercise is to break old habits of self-criticism and to establish new habits of supporting and complimenting yourself. This does not mean you cannot evaluate your behavior and improve. It means becoming aware of your thoughts and actions and using your experiences to grow while acting as a gentle and forgiving teacher for yourself. Author Stephen Levine tells people to have mercy on themselves. Be gentle with yourself and become your own best friend.

Letting Go of the Need to Control and Achieve

Most of us race around all day, feeling that we always have more to do and cannot catch up. We are frustrated because the more we try to control our lives, the more out of control we feel. Only if we are accomplishing something—improving ourselves, taking care of someone, working—do we feel worthy. In fact we feel very uncomfortable when we are not doing something.

The truth is that we are worthy even if we do nothing, simply because we have been given the gift of life. Animals spend time just lying around, doing nothing. People also have the right just to be. You are a human *being*, not a human "doing." If you can learn to feel comfortable doing nothing, you will have taken a huge step toward accepting and loving yourself.

Do this exercise alone in a quiet room. Sit comfortably and simply do nothing. Do not plan, knit, meditate, or mentally work on problems. Avoid thoughts of what you "should" be doing. Look around you. Enjoy just being. For the time you choose, you have nowhere to go, nothing to do.

If negative thoughts arise, just notice them and let them pass without judging or criticizing yourself. Simply notice your thoughts and feelings. Whatever happens is fine. Return to gazing around you.

Try this for five minutes at first, or one minute if that's all you can stand. I lasted for less than a minute on my first attempt. I became very anxious. Other people feel vulnerable and fearful. Whatever you feel is fine. Just notice your feelings—they won't kill you.

When you feel comfortable and peaceful doing nothing for fifteen minutes, you will have mastered this exercise.

Escaping from Perfectionist Prison

This can be a difficult exercise for perfectionists and workaholics. It is simply to deliberately make at least one mistake every day for a week. Yes, *every* day for a week.

Start with something small, but make it something that will be noticed. It is best if someone will discover your mistake the same day. Make mistakes at home and at work. Make mistakes around your children, your partner, your friends, your boss, or the people you supervise. Experiment with various kinds and degrees of mistakes.

Once the mistake is noticed, you may correct it. But if you want to obtain the benefit of this exercise, you cannot tell anyone that you made the mistake on purpose or as part of an exercise. Simply say you are sorry and that you will correct the situation. Nothing more.

The most important part of this exercise is to closely observe your feelings when you make the mistake and when it is discovered. How do you expect people to react? Do you expect different people to react differently? What are your assumptions about the consequences of making a mistake?

Observe how different people react to each situation and to you. Did the fact that you made a mistake make them hate you or abandon you? You may be very surprised by the results.

At the end of the week, think about what you learned

12

Resolving Issues with People Who Have Died

We find our soul when that which is most precious to us is taken away.

—**Thomas Moore,** *Care of the Soul*

Western culture does not cope well with death. We are shielded from death throughout our lives, as though having anything to do with death, even thinking about it, might somehow make it contagious.

When a loved one dies, usually alone in an antiseptic hospital room, the body is taken away as quickly as possible and strangers prepare it for burial or cremation out of the view of friends and family. Thick caskets further shelter us from the reality of death. Even when the casket is open, the body is disguised by morticians to make it look the way it did when the person was alive, concealing the truth of death. This not only makes it difficult for survivors to accept the fact of death, but deprives them of an opportunity to see that the body is merely a shell the spirit has abandoned.

I was fifty-four years old the first time I saw a dead body up close, when my mother died in a hospital. I was surprised to find that it was a great comfort to be able to touch her and kiss her goodbye. The experience was wonderful because I saw that my mother had departed, and that only a discarded shell remained. I became convinced beyond any doubt that people are not their bodies and that something transcending the physical exists after death.

Just as the body is disguised, so the survivors are encouraged to disguise their grief. Bereaved family members and friends are discouraged from crying and applauded for how well they hide their feelings—as Jackie Kennedy's example illustrates. Many well-intentioned people urge survivors to put aside their grief in a couple of weeks or months at the most, and to get on with their lives, thus truncating the grieving process.

Children are generally "protected" from death, and may learn of it only from whispers behind closed doors. One of my clients, whom I will call Joan, recovered a memory from when she was five of seeing her mother receive a telegram and start to cry. Her mother ran into the other room and shut the door. Joan knew that something terrible had happened, but no one talked to her or explained anything. She was terrified and confused. Later Joan's grandmother told her that her father had been killed in the war and that she must not disturb her mother. Joan was taken to stay with neighbors.

Joan was traumatized not only by the loss of her father, but by the emotional loss of her mother and the admonition not to cry. Since her mother did not talk to her, share her grief, or comfort her, Joan assumed that her mother somehow blamed Joan for her father's death. As a result, Joan's relationship with her mother deteriorated. The fact that Joan was also excluded from the funeral further confirmed her belief that she was being punished and was somehow responsible for the death. Joan lost both her father and mother on the same day and the effects of her family's well-intentioned attempts to "protect" her destroyed Joan's life and her relationship with her mother for more than thirty years. Only after Joan recovered these memories, released her suppressed emotions, and reexamined her beliefs about herself and her mother was she able to feel close to her mother and experience happiness and love.

Treatment of the dying is even worse in our culture, although it has improved over the years, mainly through the efforts of psychiatrist Elizabeth Kubler-Ross, the advent of hospices, and more enlightened education of medical students and other health care professionals about death and dying. Although most terminally ill patients are no longer isolated and ignored, some health care professionals still avoid contact with dying patients and "protect" them from knowledge of their condition, which prevents them from working through the grieving process and attaining peace.

In most other cultures, death and the dead are respected, even worshipped, and elaborate rituals reduce the fear of death and support survivors through the grief process. Children in these cultures are taught to accept death as part of life rather than being shielded from it, they are included in funeral ceremonies, and families openly share their grief. I find it ironic that many traditional cultures, without the benefit of extensive academic knowledge of psychology, encourage unabashed expressions of grief—acknowledging the damage caused by suppressing emotions— while we still follow our destructive stoic tradition.

The western view of death generally is one of almost total denial that ignores the psychological impact and the stages through which we must pass in order to heal. Most of us are left with "unfinished business," unresolved feelings of loss, guilt, anger, and grief, which can destroy future relationships and make subsequent losses more painful. Our society provides brief support at funerals, then leaves survivors to their own devices, with the tacit admonition to be strong and not inflict their grief on others. Small wonder that so many children and adults suffer serious trauma after someone important in their life dies.

Psychiatrist Elizabeth Kubler-Ross did much to shed light on the process of death, dying, and grieving, and described basic stages of healing through which the dying and survivors pass. These stages are shock and denial, anger, bargaining, depression and grief, and finally acceptance. Repression of emotion at any of these stages will cause pain later on.

People may go through these stages in different orders and may move back and forth from one stage to another during the process, but each stage must be experienced and resolved for a state of peace to be reached. In some cases, the natural course of this grief process may take years, but many people don't complete the process because their loved ones and friends pressure them to put the death behind them and get on with their lives. Problems frequently arise when people become stuck in the denial, anger, or grief stages, usually because they do not completely release their feelings and cannot move to another stage.

You may have unfinished business whether you loved or hated the person who died. Unfinished business means that you did not express intense emotions at the time they were evoked, you did not say something to the deceased that you wanted to express, or you have feelings of guilt about the death. Death can freeze your emotions about the deceased as they were at the moment of death. People who have expressed their feelings as they arose may have few regrets and little to repress. But most of us have unresolved feelings after someone significant dies.

The good news is that you can still resolve unfinished business and deal with unexpressed feelings after the death. This is often more difficult than it should be because feelings of anger are discouraged and people are told not to "speak ill of the dead." But healing requires you to express your anger, whether you loved or hated the deceased. If a loved one dies, you may be angry because the person left you, did not love you the way you wanted, or did not provide for you. If the deceased hurt you, you may be stuck in old anger about what was done to you and how it affected your life, or new anger because you were deprived of the chance to tell the person how you felt. In either case, you need to release your anger so that you can truly get on with your life.

The following exercises are designed to help you move through stages where you may be stuck and resolve unfinished business after a significant person in your life has died.

Accepting the Reality

Sometimes people have difficulty accepting the reality that someone has died. This technique is designed to help you accept the fact of death and release your feelings by mentally recreating the deceased's funeral.

Start by closing your eyes and using the progressive muscle relaxation technique on pages 149. When you are relaxed, picture with as much detail as possible the deceased being placed in a coffin. What do you see? What is the weather like? How does it smell? What do you hear? Who else is present? Your vision does not have to be accurate; the purpose is to evoke feelings you may have repressed.

Visualize the person in a coffin; it can be open or closed. Talk to the person in your mind or out loud and give yourself permission to let go and tell the person everything you always wanted to say: what you felt about the person when he or she was alive, what you felt about how the person treated you, how you felt when he or she died, what you think of the person now. This is the time to let all of your emotions out; you can cry, swear, and scream as loudly as you want. You may want to imagine what the person would say to you and discuss unresolved issues. You may prefer to visualize a deathbed scene so you can talk to the person while he or she is still alive. The aim is to make it all as real as possible so you can release your feelings and say goodbye.

Next, mentally follow the funeral procession to the grave. Even if the person was not actually buried, visualizing a burial helps to make the death final. When you are at the grave, say goodbye to the person and consider how you intend to live the rest of your life. Would the deceased want you to be happy or guilty and miserable? Will you let that person continue to control you from the grave by imprisoning you in anger, hatred, or guilt? Or will you break free of that hold and let your anger and guilt go, knowing you control your life now? Tell the person how you intend to live your life from now on.

Now visualize the person being buried. See the dirt covering the grave. Then imagine yourself walking away from the grave knowing that the person is dead and that you are free to live a happy life. Repeat this exercise until you feel you have accepted the death.

This exercise is even more effective if you can do it at the actual burial site.

Resolving Unfinished Business

Most people have had to face the death of a loved one or someone who played a significant role in their lives. You may regret that you did not express your feelings to your loved ones when they were alive. This exercise will help you release some of those feelings and reach closure with the deceased, a state where you understand your feelings and make peace with them in order to go on to new relationships without being burdened by the past.

Find a time when you will be undisturbed for about an hour. Sit comfortably with your eyes closed. Take a few deep breaths until you feel relaxed. You might use the progressive muscle relaxation exercise on page 149. Then picture the deceased as clearly as you can in your mind. Some people find it helpful to visualize white light surrounding the deceased. If you feel anxious, you may want to visualize a friend or religious figure with you.

Talk to the person in your mind or out loud. Tell the deceased what you feel about him or her, how he or she affected your life, and how you felt about the death. If you are feeling guilty about something, tell the person how you feel and that you are sorry. Say everything you always wanted to say, even if you are angry.

Be totally honest. Regardless of what you may have been told, it is okay to be angry at someone who is dead. It is common to be angry because a loved one left you, did not take care of him- or herself, or other reasons. Allow yourself to feel the anger and express it to the deceased.

Observe the person closely in your mind. What was this person really like? Was the person happy, secure, and confident? What do you think his or her life was like? Why might this person have acted the way he or she did?

After you have expressed all of your thoughts and feelings, sit quietly and wait for the person to respond. As strange as this may sound, you will usually have a thought or feeling that will help you better understand the situation.

Release the deceased by saying, "May you reach your highest good," or "May you be healed and be at peace."

Repeat this exercise until you feel a sense of peace when you think of the person.

If you think this is nonsense, you should know that American Indians have elaborate ceremonies for talking to their dead. They believe that they are actually in contact with the spirits of the deceased and that the deceased answer them. The Chinese and Mexicans set aside special days for honoring and communicating with their dead. Many Westerners report having startling communications from deceased loved ones using this technique. Try it and see what happens. The main purpose is to let your feelings out so you can find peace.

Overcoming Feelings of Guilt

It is common to have feelings of guilt when someone dies. People often reproach themselves because they feel they should have said or done something before the person died. Or worse, we may believe we were somehow responsible for the death.

Children almost universally believe that they somehow cause people to die, especially family members, because they are at a developmental stage where they think they cause everything that happens. Children may become angry and wish someone would die; if that person does die, the child feels responsible.

If someone important to you died when you were young, you are probably carrying around a burden of guilt that you may not be aware of consciously, but that can destroy your happiness. This exercise is designed to help you release suppressed feelings and let go of your guilt.

Sit quietly where you will not be disturbed for about an hour. Take some deep breaths to relax. You might use the progressive muscle relaxation exercise on page 149.

Think about the person who died. Picture him or her in your mind as clearly as possible. How did you feel about this person before the death? How did you feel about the death?

When you can feel some of the painful feelings, gently ask yourself whether you felt in any way responsible for the death. Let the answer float up into your mind without forcing it.

If you find that you feel responsible, use your adult self to reason with your child self. Carefully examine the circumstances of the death. Did your thoughts really kill? Did you really have the power to cause cancer or a heart attack? Both of these diseases result primarily from stress and physical deterioration over many years. One incident cannot cause cancer or a heart attack. And people who commit suicide do so out of deep feelings of self-hate and anger, not because of one or two events just prior to the suicide.

Picture the person in your mind and think about his or her life. Did you really have the control over that person you think you had? Does anyone have enough control over you to cause you to die? Use adult reasoning to convince your child self of the truth and do not stop until you feel a shift in your mind or body.

Survivors often feel guilty simply because they are still alive. We find ways to blame ourselves because we cannot find a reason for death. A dear friend of mine cared for her husband at home for many months while he was dying of a brain tumor. She rarely left his side because she did not want him to die alone. One night she told him that she was going to brush her teeth to get ready for bed and he acknowledged it with an eye signal. While she was out of the room for ten minutes, he died. My friend could not forgive herself until we discussed the fact that people often choose when they will die and wait to die alone to spare their loved ones pain.

Ask yourself whether you would forgive your loved one if the situation were reversed. Talk to yourself or with a friend until you fully understand the situation and that you did the best you could at the time.

Remembering a Loved One

In our culture, we have an unfortunate tendency to avoid talking about loved ones who have died. We encourage the bereaved to talk about other things and not to dwell on death. Although this advice is well intentioned, its effect is detrimental. An important part of healing from the loss of a loved one is reminiscing and sharing recalled stories of the loved one with family and friends. Talking about the person who has died and feelings of loss can prevent a traumatic reaction where feelings are repressed and cause damage later. It is unhealthy to refrain from talking about deceased loved ones as though they never existed. Of course, it is also unhealthy to talk about the deceased all the time to the exclusion of everything else. However, it is unrealistic to think we can ever forget a deceased partner, friend, child, parent, or other family member; that person remains a part of out lives forever.

Survivors must be encouraged to talk about people they love who have died and to remember both the good and the bad events they shared. The deceased needs to be remembered realistically. The old adage about not speaking ill of the dead has been debunked by modern psychological research. For psychological health you need to remember and speak freely about all aspects of someone who died, the bad as well as the good.

If you have lost a loved one, invite members of your family and friends to a party to talk about the deceased. Ask your guests to bring photographs they have of the loved one and to be prepared to tell stories of things they remember about him or her. What is the best time they remember? What is the worst? What did the deceased like and dislike? You and your guests need to help each other create a realistic, three-dimensional image of the deceased.

Another way to remember is by creating a ceremony or ritual to memorialize your loved one. It is unfortunate that our modern technological culture has abandoned many of the formal rituals performed by other cultures to honor and remember deceased family members and loved ones. These community rituals brought comfort and healing to our ancestors throughout the ages. To fill this void, a growing number of people are creating their own ceremonies to memorialize loved ones. Some people continue to celebrate the deceased's birthday or their wedding anniversary. After her mother's death, one woman started lighting a menorah on Hanukkah, even though she was not religious, because her mother had liked to light the candles. An annual ceremony of remembrance releases feelings of grief and loss that might otherwise accumulate during the year.

You can have fun devising creative ways to memorialize someone you love. You might plant a special garden dedicated to the deceased filled with plants or colors he or she liked. You could devote a section in your library to your loved one's favorite books. You might paint a picture of the deceased or of a place you enjoyed together, write a story, or sew a memorial quilt. You might clip pictures from magazines and make a collage depicting personality traits of your loved one or things he or she especially liked to do. Some survivors raise money for scholarships or do volunteer work in the name of their loved ones.

Completing a memorial project will give you greater feelings of closure about the death and your relationship with the deceased. But the main purpose is to do something that gives you pleasure while you think about your loved one. Isn't that what your loved one would have wanted?

13

Relaxing and Reenergizing

Be still
Listen to the stones of the wall
Be silent, they try
To speak your
Name.
Listen
To the living walls.
Who are you?
Who
Are you? Whose
Silence are you?

—Thomas Merton

We are under constant stress in our day-to-day lives. Stress is physical or mental pressure that can be positive or negative. Negative stress is tension that amounts to anxiety and results in wear and tear on the body and mind. This type of stress is the number one cause of disease and death. But stress can also be a motivating force that some therapists describe as life energy seeking to express itself. It is really not stress but *dis*tress, or stress gone bad, that causes heart attacks and other stress-related illnesses. Creative stress and hard work we enjoy can prolong life;

only negative stress kills. This chapter covers a variety of remedies for relieving the negative kind of stress and for promoting the flow of positive energy and excitement.

When people are exposed to stressful or threatening stimuli, there is an immediate biological reaction; an automatic genetic mechanism produces what is popularly called the fight-or-flight response. This response produces an increase in adrenaline, blood pressure, rate of breathing, metabolism, and heart rate. You may have seen this response in animals: cats, for instance, arch their backs and their fur stands on end when they are frightened and ready to fight or flee. The human reaction was designed to give us the ability to respond to danger by running away with extra energy or by fighting with extra strength, which we needed when we lived in caves. But neither choice is socially acceptable in our technological society. Can you imagine a frightened employee sprinting away from an intimidating employer at a staff meeting? Although we have the same amount of fear as our ancestors, we respond in more "civilized" ways (at least outwardly) as our bodies still react biologically in the primitive way predetermined by our genetic programming. Since we no longer use the stress to fight or flee, the increased adrenaline and stress remain in our systems so that the physiological changes created by this response become dangerous to the very bodies they were designed to protect.

So what can we do to protect ourselves from the impact of stress? Exercise is one way of neutralizing the harmful effects of the fight-or-flight response by using up our excess adrenaline. It is a substitute for running away or fighting. Our bodies don't care whether we are running from a saber-toothed tiger or walking in a park as long as the stress is released. The section on physical exercise on page 101 suggests some stress-releasing options.

Stress can also be released through various relaxation techniques, some of which are described in this chapter. Progressive muscle relaxation, for instance, is an easy way to quickly relieve tension and is prescribed by many therapists. This basic relaxation technique is also a simple way to reach a relaxed state before using the Inner Exploration Process, visualization, and an assortment of other therapy techniques. I highly recommend that you learn this technique because it is a tool you can use to reduce stress in many situations.

The meditation technique (page 150) takes a little longer, but it has long-term benefits and more far-reaching effects than simply releasing immediate tension. Meditation helps you learn how to calm your mind so that you experience negative stress less often. How many times have you wished for inner peace, a chance to turn off the thoughts in your mind? It is your thoughts that cause stress and suffering. Meditation can give you inner peace whenever you want it. When you meditate, you give your mind a needed vacation from the barrage of thoughts that are racing around.

Meditation not only reduces stress but has a variety of other positive side effects that will help you relax and reenergize: It can help you sleep better, increase your energy and concentration, improve your ability to learn, lower your blood pressure, and heal many stress-related ailments— *all without drugs*. Meditation has been found to lower oxygen consumption, blood pressure, and heart rate, as does sleep, but it also produces alpha waves, slower brain waves that indicate peace and contentment and are not usually present in a sleep state.

When I was working in Washington, D.C., I started meditating not for any spiritual reason but because I had such severe colitis that stomach medication no longer worked. My Harvard-trained internist said there was nothing more he could do for me and handed me a book called *The Relaxation Response* written by another Harvard physician, Herbert Benson, about meditation and its amazing physiological benefits. Even though I was skeptical, I started meditating for about ten to fifteen minutes twice a day because I was in such pain I was willing to do anything. I was amazed to find that in a few weeks, the colitis I had suffered with for years was gone.

Meditation is easy and it's free. Although meditation has been around for thousands of years, we, in our fast-paced, industrialized society, have ignored it until recently. Now many physicians and hospitals are using it not only for patients but physicians and staff. Meditation is no longer only for the mystics; Western society has finally acknowledged that the ancient Eastern wisdom works. When I had a clinical therapy practice, I routinely prescribed exercise and meditation for my clients as prerequisites for working with the Inner Exploration Process. I strongly urge you to try meditating for a month and judge the results for yourself.

Progressive Muscle Relaxation

This progressive muscle relaxation exercise is widely used by therapists to help people relax. It can be used to relieve stress or to prepare for meditation, visualization, or the Inner Exploration Process.

Start by taking a deep breath, holding it for a moment—and letting it go. Be aware of how your body relaxes as you exhale. Take another couple of deep breaths and notice how your body feels as it lets go of tension when you exhale.

Now begin to focus on your feet, becoming aware of how they feel and noticing any tension. Inhale and, as you breathe out, let go of all of the tension in your feet. Feel your feet relaxing and becoming warm and comfortable. You may wish to repeat this process a couple of times until you are satisfied that the tension has been reduced (it is not necessary to remove every bit of tension). You might imagine that you are inhaling peace and that your breath is traveling to the part you are relaxing.

When you have let go of the tension in your feet, notice how your calves and knees feel and, as you exhale, let go of any tension in your calves and knees. Feel any tension flowing out with your breath. Then become aware of any tension in your thighs and allow it to flow out with your breath. Notice your legs relaxing and becoming warm and comfortable. Continue up your body, releasing any tension in each part; your pelvis, abdomen, chest, back, hands, arms, shoulders, neck, face, and head. You can focus on combinations of body parts or separate them further if you store your tension in a particular area I have not mentioned, such as your fingers.

Then do a quick scan of your whole body for any remaining areas of tension. Breathe peace and calm into those areas and permit yourself to let go of the tension as you exhale. Scan your body again and enjoy the increased feeling of comfort and relaxation which you have created for yourself.

A variation of this exercise involves tensing and relaxing the muscles of each area of your body. For example, when you focus on your feet, tense your feet, really tighten them, curl your toes, and hold them that way for a few seconds. Now relax your feet, letting all the tension go. Feel the relaxation in your feet, the comfort and warmth tingling in them.

Let this feeling of relaxation move up into your calves and knees, and then tighten the muscles in your calves and knees, as tight as you can (without ever being uncomfortable or hurting yourself), feeling the tension you have created. Now let go, and feel your muscles relax; notice the wonderful tingling sensation of comfort and warmth. Follow this sensation up into your thighs and repeat the process, tensing and releasing every part of your body, just as you did with the first exercise. Be sure to pay particular attention to your back, neck, shoulders, and face, especially your jaw, since many people hold tension in these areas.

When you have moved from toes to head, scan your body for any remaining areas of tension and tense and release those places. Notice how your body feels and thank yourself for the feeling of comfort and relaxation you have given to yourself.

Meditation Made Simple

Meditation can reduce stress, increase your energy and concentration, improve your health, help you sleep better, and more. Physicians in the United States have finally accepted the results of scientific studies revealing the benefits of meditation and are prescribing it for their patients. Many corporations are hiring highly paid trainers to teach meditation to their employees. However, meditation is simple and you can learn to do it without a guru or expensive courses.

Find a quiet place where you will not be disturbed for twenty minutes. Once you become used to meditating, you can do it anywhere—in buses, jets, or at dull parties, but in the beginning you'll need peace and quiet. Sit comfortably with your spine straight, but do not lie down because you may fall asleep.

It is best to meditate where you will not be interrupted because if something disturbs you, you may feel like you have been jerked awake from a nap and left with a jangled feeling. Although one purpose of meditation is to clear your mind of thoughts, you remain aware of your surroundings and can answer a phone or respond coherently if someone speaks to you.

Choose something to focus on. Mentally repeating a mantra—a word, a line from a prayer, or a statement that is meaningful to you—is the most effective way to clear your mind of thoughts. Whether you choose a line or phrase from a prayer or a single word such as "love," "one," or "peace," the results are the same. The purpose of these words is to give your mind a focus so you will not be distracted by outside disturbances or your thoughts.

Most people find it easier to ignore distractions by closing their eyes, but other people keep their eyes open, focusing on a beautiful object or a blank wall. Do whatever works best for you.

Use deep breathing or the progressive muscle relaxation exercise on page 149 to relax. Then focus on breathing through your nose and each time you exhale, think in your mind the word or phrase you have chosen. For example, inhale and then as you exhale think the word "peace," and repeat this pattern throughout the period of meditation. Breathe naturally and slowly.

If thoughts intrude, and they will, first acknowledge the thought and then simply let it drift away, returning your focus to your word or phrase. Do not fight thoughts or try to force them out of your mind. It is normal to have thoughts; just notice them without judgment and let them float through your mind.

If you are distracted or anxious, you may want to repeat your word in your mind both as you inhale and exhale. You will find your thoughts decreasing the longer you practice meditation. Don't worry about thoughts intruding; studies show you are still benefitting.

The optimum time for meditating is ten to twenty minutes once or twice a day. It is better to wait an hour or more after meals before meditating. If you fall asleep while meditating, do not worry about it. Your body needed the rest.

At first the time may seem endless and you may find yourself constantly checking your watch. After a few weeks, you will find that you no longer have to check the time. Time may seem to pass quickly and your eyes will open automatically after ten or twenty minutes when your body has reached an optimal state of relaxation.

Come out of meditation gently, taking two or three minutes to become alert before you start moving. If you stand up quickly you may get dizzy, just as if you stood up abruptly from a nap. Get up slowly, inhaling as you stand. Savor the peace you have attained for yourself.

Nothing specific is supposed to happen when you meditate, except that you become more relaxed. Everyone has his or her own particular experience. So don't worry about whether you are achieving the "proper" state. Just continue to practice meditation for a month or so and you will begin to notice an increasing sense of peace.

An optional step after you stop meditating and before resuming your daily activities is to focus your mind for another five or ten minutes on something positive; a poem, a passage from a self-help book, a prayer, or even a happy picture. By concentrating on something positive, you are imprinting that idea in your brain while it is in a receptive state.

Relieving Stress Quickly

This is an exercise for relieving tension quickly. It may make you laugh because it seems rather silly. You will usually want to do this exercise in private, but it can also be fun with your children, partner, or close friends.

Stand and write your full name in the air with your nose. Yes, that's what I mean: Pretend your nose is a pencil and draw the letters of your name in the air, moving your head and neck as loosely as possible.

When you have finished, write your name again—this time with your behind. Draw the letters as large and freely as you can, moving your whole body.

It's okay to laugh. Laughter is the best way to relieve stress.

Energized Prayer

The most powerful technique I have found is prayer. My prayers for guidance, courage, understanding, forgiveness, or help in my personal growth have almost always been fulfilled. And prayer has worked for me in many other ways.

There are no rules for praying. I believe prayers should be simple, honest, and direct—from the heart. I usually add "if it's in my best interest and the best interest of the universe," to my prayers because I do not want to ask for something that is not good for me—or prevent myself from receiving something even better.

Sometimes a simple, "Thy will be done," may be the most effective prayer, surrendering to the realization that God, love, and the universe are benevolent and always working for our highest good. Use whatever feels right for you.

When I cannot deal with my feelings or have a problem I think I cannot handle, I simply offer them up to a higher power and ask to have the situation resolved. Usually the feelings diminish and an answer comes within a day or two, sometimes through a person, other times through a book or something I see on television.

Prayers have more energy when we are under stress—when we really need them. Studies of the effects of prayer on plants show that where plants were given the same water, light, and food, the group of plants that were prayed for by people miles away grew twice as fast as plants that did not receive prayers. In a second experiment, salt, which is damaging to plants and can kill them, was placed in all the pots. In this case, the group of plants that people prayed for grew *four times* larger than the other plants. My experience is the same: the more I have needed help, the better my prayers have worked.

If prayer is so effective, why bother with any of the other exercises in this book? The answer may be found in an Arab saying: "Trust in God, but tie up your camel." God may guide and support us, but we have choices. You have free will and are responsible for your own healing. And you can heal yourself in many ways.

Golden Sun-Guided Imagery

Scientists say that we need fifteen to twenty minutes of direct sunlight every day, not filtered through windows, in order to maintain good health. To avoid harmful ultraviolet rays, it is best to do this exercise before 11 A.M. or after 2 P.M. A perfect time would be your morning or afternoon break.

Lie or sit comfortably in the sun for ten or fifteen minutes and feel the warmth on your body. (You may want to set an alarm clock so you don't fall asleep and stay out too long.) Close your eyes and notice how the sun feels on various parts of your body. Imagine the sun's gentle golden rays surrounding you, flowing through your body, bringing you to perfect health. Picture the golden light filling your body until every muscle, every organ, every atom of your body is filled with gentle golden light. See yourself as totally filled with radiant, golden light.

A variation of this exercise can also be used inside on a rainy day. Although you will not have the benefit of the sun's rays, doing this exercise on chilly days will help you feel warmer.

Sit or lie down, close your eyes, and relax. Imagine a brilliant golden sun above you. Imagine the warmth of the sun on your body. Then picture the golden light filling your body as described above.

You can also use a variation of this exercise to help you feel warmer on cold days. Practice it while you are walking outdoors or waiting for a bus. Imagine that there is a large, hot, yellow-orange ball of light in your chest. Visualize the heat of the ball spreading through your chest. Feel the warmth spread throughout the rest of your body all the way to the tips of your fingers and down to your toes. Continue to intensify the feeling of warmth spreading to every part of your body. The results may surprise you.

Sleeping Aids

How can you fall asleep more easily—without taking pills? Research shows that while prescription and over-the-counter medications may help you sleep the night you take them, they disrupt your normal sleep patterns and may create worse problems, such as addiction, increased insomnia, nightmares, and even psychosis. There are many safer ways to help you fall asleep.

Most doctors recommend exercising in the afternoon or early evening, a light dinner, and some kind of relaxation before bedtime. Avoid watching violent shows on television—especially the nightly news— before going to bed; watching or reading about acts of violence causes tension and fear, stimulating an adrenaline reaction. Instead, read soothing or inspirational material or listen to relaxing music. If you do watch television, choose a comedy or nature program just before going to bed.

Take a warm bath or shower, or have a massage before going to bed, and make sure you are warm and comfortable wherever you sleep. If your feet are cold, wear socks or warm your bed with a heating pad or hot-water bottle. Some people find it helpful to wear a sleep mask to eliminate light or earplugs to reduce noise; both are available at pharmacies. If over-the-counter earplugs are not adequate, you can have customized ear plugs made for you at an ear clinic.

If you have insomnia, establish regular sleeping patterns; go to bed at the same time each night. Some people do not sleep well in bedrooms; you might try sleeping in another room or on a different kind of bed.

Warm milk has been discovered to be one of the most effective sleeping potions. It seems that milk contains a natural sleep-inducing chemical. If you can't stand the taste of milk, add some honey or a sprinkle of nutmeg. Avoid cocoa, which contains stimulants.

Think pleasant thoughts, remember happy times with friends and loved ones, picture beautiful places in your mind.

If you still can't sleep, do not stay in bed and worry about it. Get up and read, write a letter to a friend, or enjoy your favorite hobby, listen to relaxing music—anything that is not stressful. Go back to bed when you start to feel sleepy.

You may need less sleep than you think. Some studies show we only need five hours of sleep a night to function efficiently and maintain our health, so you may already be getting all the sleep you need. Albert Einstein only slept three hours a night and took short naps during the day. Many people who have difficulty sleeping at night find it helpful to nap during the day. When I worked in an office, I used to tell my secretary not to disturb me, curl up on the floor, and sleep for fifteen or twenty minutes. Now I take nap breaks at home to help myself work more productively.

Chronic insomnia can be a symptom of post-traumatic stress disorder and may be relieved by uncovering and resolving the underlying trauma. Soldiers who experienced enemy attacks at night often have sleep disorders, as do people who are worried about problems they may not be dealing with consciously. Children who were molested at night frequently have difficulty sleeping at night.

Most people find that their problems with getting to sleep improve once they uncover the causes of their sleep disorder, release their suppressed emotions, and convince their child selves that they are now safe. Use the Inner Exploration Process to find out if past events are causing the sleep problems. When you are relaxed, simply ask your mind to show you memories or to give you information about why you have difficulty sleeping. If you uncover memories of severe trauma and are unable to resolve them yourself, seek the help of a professional. Your sleep disorder can be cured.

The regular practice of meditation (page 150) will also help you feel more rested and improve your ability to sleep. And you can try techniques to help you sleep once you are in bed. One is the progressive muscle relaxation exercise on page 149. The other I call "Sandbag." This exercise can be used alone or after the progressive relaxation exercise.

Sandbag

The Sandbag exercise works better if you are lying on your back but you can do it on your side or stomach. Get into a comfortable position; wiggle until your body feels just right. Become aware of your body lying on the bed. Feel the sheets above and below you and focus on how your whole body feels supported by the mattress.

Imagine that your body is completely filled with fine grains of sand. How does it feel to be completely stuffed with sand—in your legs, torso, arms, and head? Feel the heaviness, the weight pushing you into the mattress.

Now imagine that someone is painlessly poking holes all around your body and that the sand is starting to pour slowly out of you. Focus on an arm or leg and feel the sand flowing out of many small holes. Feel yourself deflating, becoming lighter and lighter. Focus on your other arm, then your legs, torso and head, imagining the sand pouring out. Feel the sand flowing out of your whole body. Feel your whole body deflating, relaxing, becoming lighter and lighter. Feel the sand gently pouring out as you become lighter and lighter, hardly feeling your body.

Keep focusing on the sand flowing out as you fall asleep.

You might tape record this exercise in a quiet, slow voice, directing your attention to individual parts of your body. When you are comfortably in bed at night, play the tape on a machine that shuts off automatically.

14

Creating a New Vision of Your Future and Getting What You Want

Whatever you
> *Vividly imagine*
> *Ardently desire*
> *Firmly believe and*
> *Enthusiastically act upon*
Must inevitably come to pass.

—John Buckley

An important part of healing is the ability to believe in and create a positive future for yourself. You are responsible for creating the future you want, and, once you eliminate your limiting beliefs, the possibilities are infinite. As difficult as it may be to believe right now, whatever you want to change you can. No matter what you have suffered in the past and no matter what "personality" traits you believe you have, you can change your life and your personality. The Inner Exploration Process and other techniques in this book are designed to help you become more aware of beliefs and behaviors that may be sabotaging your happiness so you can eliminate them. This chapter focuses on techniques to help you discover what you really want and ways to get it.

You have to know what you want in order to be able to get it. If you don't know what you want, you just take what comes along. Corporations recognize the importance of goal-setting, not just for individuals but for the productivity of the whole organization; they spend thousands of dollars every year on meetings and retreats where executives and employees create mission statements for the corporation and its departments, because having goals increases productivity and profitability.

The goal-setting exercise in this chapter is a synthesis of various exercises taught in expensive seminars for corporate executives. It will help you discover exactly what you want and set your priorities, so you can start achieving your goals. The other exercises provide some tools to make it easier for you to achieve these goals.

Setting New Goals

People who have clear goals are more successful and happier than those who just go along day by day. If you don't know what you want, it's hard to be successful. This exercise will help you clarify your long- and short-term goals. Focusing on the results you want will help you find ways to succeed.

This is a goal-setting exercise that people pay hundreds of dollars to learn at executive training conferences. You can do it for yourself at home.

You will need a pencil with an eraser, eight or more sheets of paper, and a couple of hours free of interruptions.

On the first sheet, write "Long-Term Life Goals," and make a list of all the general long-term goals that come to mind: financial security, happiness, personal growth, a loving relationship, success, and so on.

Then write the following categories at the top of separate pages:

- Physical/Health
- Intellectual/Education
- Emotional
- Spiritual
- Relationships
- Work/Financial

On each page, first list as many long-term goals in that category as you can and then your short-term goals. Start each goal with "My goal is . . ." This will help you eliminate unimportant goals.

Then choose one general long-term goal and three of the more specific short-term goals in each category. Erase or cross out the others. For "Physical/Health," your long-term goal may be to become healthier, take better care of yourself, or lose weight. Short-term goals might be to reduce your sugar intake, exercise regularly, learn to roller blade, or get your teeth straightened.

Put down exactly what you *want*, not what you think you should have or can achieve. The sky is the limit here. I believe you can have, do, and be whatever you want. This belief is confirmed each time one-legged skiers fly by me down the mountain.

Last, review your list of "Long-Term Life Goals" and add to it. Then pick one life goal, erase the rest, and write your goal at least three times as a positive statement: "I have financial security," "I am loved," or "I am happy."

Review all of your goals the following day and change whatever you wish. On each page, jot down specific actions you might take to achieve each of your goals. Don't worry if you can't think of any specifics right away. Simply having a goal will help you recognize opportunities as they arise.

One of your goals might be to take one small step each day or each week toward one or two of your goals. Be gentle with yourself; don't expect to attain all your goals immediately.

Read over your goals at least once a month. Many people carry their list of goals in their day planner or wallet. The more you read your goals, the more firmly you plant them in your mind. Keeping your goals in mind also helps you make choices and set your daily priorities.

Add or change any of your goals at any time. When the new year rolls around, you may be surprised at what you have accomplished.

Visualizing New Possibilities

This exercise will help you improve your ability to visualize. If you cannot visualize having what you want, it is difficult to get it. The ability to picture clearly what you want attracts what you want to you by allowing you to create opportunities and helping you see them when they come. Many Olympic athletes visualized winning their gold medals long before they competed in the games, as did six-time Olympic gold medalist Mark Spitz. You need to be able to imagine new possibilities in order to create and receive them in your life.

For a long time, I was unable to visualize having a happy, loving, gentle relationship with a man. My mental pictures, based on past experiences, would deteriorate into scenes of conflict and fights. My intimate relationships were disastrous. Now that I am well along in my healing and have found role models for good relationships, I am better able to imagine the kind of relationship I want for myself, and my relationships have improved immeasurably.

Many people have difficulty visualizing, but everyone has the ability to do it. This exercise will help you hone your abilities so that you can picture people, objects, and situations clearly.

Close your eyes, take a few deep breaths, and imagine a bright red apple in front of your eyes. Picture the shape and the color as vividly as you can. If you do not see anything, place a red apple in front of you and observe it for a few minutes with your eyes open. Then close your eyes and picture the apple in your mind. Try this with other objects.

When you can mentally see the apple and other objects, picture a friend standing in front of you. Imagine the friend laughing, walking toward you, walking away from you.

Another exercise is to imagine a blank television or movie screen. Now picture characters or a scene from your favorite program on the screen.

Imagine the sound of a bird, a flock of birds, a dog barking, a car horn.

Picture yourself lifting a heavy object, walking down a long flight of stairs, rocking gently in a rowboat floating down a stream.

Imagine how you would feel if you were happy, sad, angry, scared.

Imagine the taste of a juicy lemon, the taste of chocolate.

Imagine the smell of a rose, gasoline, smoke, toast.

Imagine the warmth of a hot shower, the texture of velvet, the texture of rough sandpaper.

Imagine a peaceful, green meadow. Now imagine it filled with multi-colored wildflowers. Feel the warmth of the sun on your skin. Feel a slight breeze blowing your hair. Smell the scent of flowers or pine trees in your mind.

Few people will be able to visualize all of these clearly, but you can increase your ability to visualize by carefully observing the sights, sounds, smells, textures, and tastes you experience and doing your best to remember them. Practice recreating them in your mind.

Recognizing Your Strengths

This exercise will help you focus on the qualities that make you special and valuable. Most people spend much more time worrying about their weaknesses than concentrating on their strengths. Recognizing your gifts improves your self-esteem.

Find a time when you can spend thirty minutes or so uninterrupted. You will need paper and a pen or pencil. Write "My Strengths" in large letters at the top of the page and then divide the page into five columns.

Label the first column "Physical" and list all the positive things about your health, appearance, body, and physical ability. Describe each attribute in a couple of words rather than long sentences. For example: curly hair, warm smile, straight teeth, exercise regularly, good eyesight, run fast, good skier, and so on.

The next column is "Mental Abilities" and might include learning quickly, curiosity, reading, and skills such as operating computers, or working with numbers.

The third category covers your "Emotional" strengths: being warm, sensitive, compassionate, and honest.

Fourth is "Friendship," what you have to offer as a friend: loyalty, kindness, understanding, listening, fun, and so on.

Last is "Intimate Relationships," what you have to offer a partner: affection, caring, support, comfort, sensuality, money (yes, the ability to provide financial security and nice things is a positive attribute), or laughter.

As you make your list, you may find yourself thinking of faults or qualities you lack. We are all growing; no one has only strengths. Tell yourself that it's okay to be imperfect—you're human—and gently bring your mind back to your strengths. Describe what you *are*, not what you've done. If you find it helpful to recall things you've accomplished, create a sixth category for "Accomplishments" you are proud of.

When you finish, go over your list again and add anything you might have missed. Then put your list aside and review it again the next day, adding other thoughts. Continue to review and add to your list once a week—or at least once a month—until you have your positive attributes clearly in mind. Save your list and refer to it whenever you begin to feel inadequate.

Creating Confidence

This exercise will help you meet new situations and challenges with confidence.

Sit quietly with your spine straight, close your eyes, and take several deep breaths. Keep breathing deeply, focusing on your breath until you feel relaxed.

Remember a time when you felt successful, totally in control, when everything was going your way. If you think of more than one incident, focus on the one you can remember most vividly including your feelings at the time. Picture in your mind all of the circumstances: what did you do, how did you act, and most importantly, how did you feel when you succeeded?

Feel all of the sensations in your mind and body. How did your head feel, your chest, your stomach, your legs? Imagine feeling that way now. Mentally picture yourself, your surroundings, and any other people who were present. What were you wearing? What was the temperature? What sounds did you hear? What did you smell? Did you move or speak in a certain way? See yourself move and talk that way now.

When you vividly reexperience your feelings of success, press the thumb and middle finger of your right hand together firmly, and hold them together for a minute.

Repeat this exercise a couple of times on different days.

The next time you feel anxious and want to feel more confident, press your thumb and middle finger together; you will remember how it felt to be successful. Concentrate on those feelings until your anxiety dissipates.

Tapping the Power of Your Subconscious Mind

This exercise will show you how to invoke the power of your subconscious mind to achieve positive results. It will give you proof that your subconscious mind follows the instructions of your conscious mind and makes them a reality.

Try this when you have mislaid something, such as your keys, wallet, or glasses. Observe yourself as you search for the object. What are you saying to yourself? Most people repeat, "I can't find my keys," or "I can't remember where I put my keys," out loud or in their minds.

When you have searched without success, stop. Take a few deep breaths and relax for a minute. Then say to yourself several times in your mind, "I know exactly where my keys are and I will find them quickly and easily." You do not have to believe what you are saying. By repeating the positive statement in your mind, you are directing your subconscious to accept it. Just keep repeating the positive statement as you resume your search and see what happens.

The results are usually amazing. Most people will go directly to the object they are looking for.

Your subconscious mind is like a giant computer, accepting what you tell it without analyzing or judging. Only your conscious mind analyzes and judges what you think. Your conscious mind tells your subconscious mind what to think and do. Each time you say, "I can't find my keys," your conscious mind is telling your subconscious mind *not* to find your keys and you may overlook them even if they are in plain sight.

When you say to yourself that you know where something is and will find it quickly and easily, you are directing your subconscious mind to use all of your faculties to do just that.

This programming works in all areas of life. If you are skiing and tell yourself that a slope is too steep and you will fall, you probably will. But if you repeat in your mind, "This is easy," you will find that it is.

Experiment with repeating positive statements in your mind whenever you think you cannot do something or that it will be difficult. You may discover the true power of your mind.

Establishing Healthy Boundaries

Many people find it difficult to protect themselves in threatening situations because they become immobilized by fear. This exercise is designed to help you break out of patterns of victimization and establish healthy boundaries.

You will need a friend to help with this exercise, someone with whom you feel safe. Ask your friend to stand ten or fifteen feet away, facing you. Have your friend walk toward you while you remain stationary. When your friend reaches a point near you where you feel uncomfortable, put your arms straight out in front of you with your palms facing your friend and say "Stop!" You must say "Stop!" in an authoritative adult voice, without laughing or sounding like a child. Ask your friend to tell you whether you look and sound firm and convincing.

Do not allow your friend to get closer to you than an arm's length before you put out your hands. Your arms should be stretched to their full length, palms facing outward without touching your friend. But do not put your arms out too soon. The ideal distance from your friend is about a foot from your hands.

Repeat this exercise until you feel strong and confident. If you sound timid or childlike, try shouting "Stop!" as loudly as you can until you feel more powerful. Then decrease the volume. The object is to bring the power of your voice up from your diaphragm so that you sound forceful without shouting. You may feel or sound angry or fearful at first. Repeat the process until the anger and fear disappear and you can say "Stop!" in a forceful but calm manner.

When you feel confident and comfortable putting your hands up and staying "Stop!" and your friend finds your actions convincing, have your friend run toward you in an angry or threatening way, and repeat the process until you can say "Stop!" in a convincing way.

The final step is to put your arms out and say "Stop!" convincingly when your friend runs toward you waving his or her arms threateningly and yelling the terrible things someone you fear said to you as a child. It should be clear that under no circumstances will your friend harm you.

You may want to change roles with your friend and repeat the three steps.

This exercise can bring out strong emotions and unexpected reactions. Many people become numb and are unable to move when someone moves toward them in a threatening manner. Others cry. Some men tend to become angry and use force. The purpose of this exercise is to become aware of how you react in threatening situations so you can change your automatic reactions and protect yourself.

If you find this exercise difficult or unpleasant, you need to do it. You may have to repeat it for several weeks before you are able to stop someone convincingly and feel really comfortable.

Learning to Say "No"

This exercise will help you set boundaries and take care of your own needs. Many people, especially women, are people pleasers. They have been conditioned to take care of everyone else's needs, and to deny and neglect their own. You may feel compelled to do things for others you really don't want to do, and then you wonder why you're filled with anger and resentment. Some people deny their own needs because they misinterpret the biblical admonition, "Love thy neighbor as thyself." They think it means to put others first, overlooking the pivotal word "as," which indicates that love is supposed to be equal for all. You must learn to love and take care of yourself before you can love and take care of others.

This exercise is simple—you just say "No," out loud in an assertive, authoritative, adult, and convincing way. Keep repeating "No," until it becomes easy and you feel comfortable and powerful saying it. If you have any doubts about being persuasive, continue saying "No!" Shout it over and over at the top of your lungs. Then tone it down to a strong, firm tone you could use in public. You should feel your voice and power coming from deep down in your abdomen.

Some people feel so uncomfortable saying "no" that they may need to write it a number of times before saying it.

When you are comfortable saying "no" in a convincing way by yourself, do this exercise with a friend or partner. Take turns saying "No" to each other until you are both comfortable and agree that the way you say "no" is adult, firm, absolute, and convincing. No laughing, explaining, or apologizing.

Make sure you look directly into the other person's eyes when you say "no" and that your body language does not contradict what you are saying. Ask each other questions or to do things that can be refused. Stop only when you and your friend or partner are sure that you will both be taken seriously when you say "no."

Practice saying no in as many circumstances as possible. Pick something easy at first, perhaps a telephone solicitation. Just say, "No. Goodbye." Hang up without any apology. You don't have to apologize to someone for disturbing you and trying to make you buy something you don't want. Then practice on people closer to you so that you can say no in a loving but firm way.

Saying "No" and Making It Stick

Have you ever felt powerless and angry because others are able to "talk you into anything?" Did you give up what you wanted to avoid a prolonged argument? The following technique will keep you from being pushed into doing things you don't want to do.

Next time you are asked to do something you'd rather not do, just say "No," without any explanation. If you are asked "Why?" simply say, "I don't want to." You don't have to justify your desires; you are entitled to them whatever they are. If you say you "can't" do something, you can be drawn into arguments about why you can or should. It's difficult for people to argue with what you want.

To avoid being dragged into tangential issues, just keep repeating "No," in a firm but pleasant way. Don't explain or respond to arguments or questions. It's hard to argue with someone who won't participate. If the other person is used to lengthy arguments, he or she may become frustrated and angry when you don't respond in the usual way. Don't back down. Simply say, "I don't want to argue with you; the answer is no."

Use this exercise carefully. If you are talking to a friend or loved one, you may want to express your feelings, leaving an opening to negotiate and discuss alternative solutions. You may temper your refusal by saying, "No, I don't want to _____ , but I'd like to _____ ," or "No, but I'd be willing to do it next week" or "No, but let's try to find an alternative solution."

If anyone, even a friend or partner, asks you to do something you don't want to do, be honest. You cannot have a successful intimate relationship if you cover up your real feelings. In the long run, relationships fail when people hide their feelings and constantly say or do what they assume others want. Continually doing things you don't want to do causes resentment, which will eventually explode into anger. The irony is that more often than not, assumptions about what others want are wrong. If you make your true feelings known and check out your assumptions, you may find there are ways to work things out so that both of you can be happy.

People who love each other want their loved ones to be happy. They don't want pretense and they don't want to force their loved ones into unwanted choices.

If you don't want to do something but are willing to do it because you think it is especially important to a loved one, take responsibility for that choice and be truthful about it. Say: "I don't want to do that, but if it's really important to you, I'm willing to do it." Then do whatever you have agreed to cheerfully, without resentment, knowing you have made a conscious choice. Don't expect anything in return. Make it clear to your loved ones that you want them to be equally honest with you.

If you begin to feel that you are making all the concessions in a relationship, express your feelings and see whether things change. If not, you have to decide if you want to continue to do all the giving.

Asking for What You Want

After you are comfortable saying "No," it's time to start asking for what you want. You may be so used to taking care of others that you find it difficult to express your own desires. This exercise is to practice asking for what you want.

Start with something simple. Ask a loved one or friend for a hug. You may be surprised at the reaction.

Don't expect people to know what you want. Practice asking for things directly: "I want to go out for dinner tonight"; "I want to make love in the living room in front of a fire"; "I just want to talk to you for a while"; "Please drive the carpool tomorrow"; "I want you just to hold me"; or "I want to be alone for a while to read."

If you don't believe this works, watch your dog or cat. Pets ask for exactly what they want, and they usually get it. My dog makes a certain sound when she wants her chest rubbed. If I scratch her head, she pushes my hand down to her chest. We humans are more subtle—and often are disappointed because we don't get what we want.

Do you believe that wanting something for yourself is selfish? Do you usually put the needs of others first, saying to yourself, "Oh, I wish I had _____. No, I really don't need that"? If this hits home, you have work to do. You need to start valuing yourself. You are special and deserve to have your needs fulfilled.

If you don't know what you want, take the time to sit quietly and think about it. You have to know what you want in order to get it. Make a list of all the things you really want, large and small, even if you think they are unrealistic. What would make you feel more loved, comfortable, less stressed, and healthier? Practice asking for those things.

If you want a special gift, don't hint about it and take the chance that you will be disappointed. Ask for it specifically: "I would really like a purple ski parka for my birthday." People who love you want to give you what you want.

Ask for what you want with the belief that you are worthy to receive it and that people will give it to you. Visualize receiving what you want before you ask for it. Picture in your mind the person you ask saying "Of course!" and being delighted to give you what you want. Or say to yourself just before you ask, "I am valuable, I deserve this, and I know I will get it."

You may not get everything you ask for, but that's all right. At least you'll have made your wishes known. The more you practice, the easier it will become.

15

Enjoying Each Moment

On Arturo Toscanini's eightieth birthday, someone asked his son, Walter, what his father ranked as his most important achievement. The son replied, "For him there can be no such thing. Whatever he happens to be doing at the moment is the biggest thing in his life—whether it is conducting a symphony or peeling an orange."

—Ardis Whitman

Most of us are so caught up in our work, worries, and concerns with simply surviving that we tend to overlook the pleasures—and the miracles—that are all around us. You need to balance clearing your past with learning to enjoy every present moment. The techniques in this chapter will help you focus on the present and the wonders that are present in each and every moment. Only the present moment really exists. The rest is illusion, because the past is gone and the future does not yet exist. The present moment is the only *real* moment; learn to relish as many moments as you can.

Living in the Present Moment

Many of us spend our waking moments regretting the past or worrying about the future. Or we race around, trying to get things done, not realizing that the joy is in the doing. Our "motion sickness" makes us mindless, rather than mindful.

This ancient technique, known as mindfulness meditation, will help you to become aware of the present moment and give you greater freedom of action by releasing you from your obsessive thoughts, worries, and fears. Through this technique, you can learn to become a detached observer of your thoughts and feelings by acknowledging them for what they are and letting them go.

Sit comfortably, close your eyes, and relax. As you start your mindfulness meditation, notice your breathing. Each time you exhale, notice how you let go of your breath and your tension.

Focus your attention on the tip of your nose and feel your breath entering and leaving your nostrils. Feel your breath going in and out of your nostrils. After a moment, just let yourself be aware of your breath as it leaves your nostrils. Throughout this meditation, keep your attention focused on your nostrils as you exhale each breath.

Observe your thoughts and feelings as they enter your mind. Don't try to suppress them, because what you resist persists. One purpose of this exercise is to become aware of your thoughts and feelings. As they come up, just notice what type of thoughts and feelings you have and label them. For example if you have the thought, "My stomach is growling and it's almost time for dinner," you might label this "hunger"; "I'll never get all my work done," you could label "worry" or "job"; and "My foot hurts," would be "pain." After you have labeled the thought, return your attention back to your breath.

Avoid judging your thoughts; be a detached observer. It may help to say in your mind, "Ah, that's a hunger thought"; "Ah, that's a sex thought"; or "Ah, that's another worry thought." If strong emotions come up, simply observe them and let them flow through you.

Mindfulness meditation should be performed for fifteen or twenty minutes once or twice a day depending on your schedule and what feels comfortable to you. The more you practice, the more peaceful and in control of your thoughts you will feel.

Relish the Now

In addition to mindfulness meditation, there are a number of simple exercises to make you more mindful, more aware of the present moment. One is eating mindfully. Eat an almond or an orange slowly, biting off small pieces and chewing slowly, enjoying the taste. Touch it, smell it, and feel its texture. Do this during meals when you can. Your parents may have told you not to play with your food, but do it anyway; you're an adult now and can do what you want.

Another of my favorite mindful exercises is bracketing moments. We rush from task to task all day without pausing to change pace. This exercise requires that you take minibreaks during the day, each time you complete a task or activity. By pausing between activities, you have a chance to focus your thoughts and energy so that you can become aware of what you accomplished and begin to focus on what you will do next. If you pause for even a minute or two, you will find you are more relaxed and better able to concentrate on your next activity.

Plan a day of mindfulness, a day when you have no schedule or things you "should" do. It is best to do this alone. Walk mindfully, observing how your body feels as you move. Feel each muscle working, how each part of your foot feels as it touches the ground. Notice the details of your surroundings, the temperature, the air on your face, sounds and smells. Do every task mindfully, even washing dishes. Feel the suds, enjoy the tiny rainbows in soap bubbles, feel the surface of the plates after they are washed. Focus totally on what you are doing. Use all of your senses to the fullest. Whatever you do, plan to spend at least twice as much time as usual doing the task. Remember the Simon and Garfunkel song: "Slow down, you move too fast, got to make the morning last."

Children, animals, and dying people are mindful; they live for the moment. People who are dying are no different from the rest of us. It is just that they have accepted the truth. We are all dying—all terminal. Each moment is all any of us has for certain. We have to learn to enjoy every one.

Creating New Experiences

At some time in their lives, most people get into a rut. Without realizing it, they become set in their routines and do the same things day after day, week after week. One way to rekindle an interest in life is to do something new every day, or at least every week.

You may want to start by varying your normal routine: take a different route to work, school, or the market; go to a new restaurant and eat exotic food you've never tried; have a picnic lunch in a local park; attend a place of worship with beliefs different from yours; watch a television program you have never seen; buy a game and play it with your family instead of watching television; rent a self-improvement or inspirational video.

Many people do only what they learned to do as children. Try new activities and see what you like. Take a hot-air balloon ride; scuba dive; get a massage; attend a lecture on a subject you know nothing about; go to a planetarium, an aura reading, or a Star Trek convention. Most cities have monthly newspapers that list all types of lectures, concerts, healing sessions, and classes, many of which are free. Try some of the ones that seem the weirdest to you—you may have fun.

Don't play it safe. Do something you think you could never do. Richard Bolles, author of the classic job-hunting book, *What Color Is Your Parachute?*, recommends interviewing people to see if you might like their jobs. You can go a step further. Pretend you are a freelance writer and interview someone you have always wanted to meet. You might even write an article about it. If you can read this book, you can write.

Make a commitment to learn something new, something you have always wanted to try, just for yourself—a skill, craft, art form, musical instrument, dance, language, or subject. Community colleges and adult education programs have a fascinating assortment of classes. Try a few and see what really interests you.

You don't have to do it well. Just have fun.

Never Be Lonely

Make a new friend.

Most of us rarely make time for the friends we have and don't make an effort to find new ones. But friends move, drift away, or die, and we often find ourselves without a support system when we need one.

Start today. Make a commitment to devote a certain amount of time each day or each week to developing friendships. Find as many ways as you can to get to know people. Not just people who have the potential to be close friends, but people who you think are really different from you. Ask neighbors or work acquaintances to lunch. Invite the parents of your child's friends over with the children, or arrange to go to the movies or a lecture. Join groups or attend classes and workshops where you can meet people with similar interests. Volunteer to work a couple of hours a month for a cause you support.

Don't expect too much from any one friend. One person cannot fulfill all your needs. One friend may like the same movies, another may be open to talking about deep personal concerns, another may enjoy sports. Accept and enjoy what each friend has to offer.

No one can always be there for you, but if you have many friends, someone will be.

Having Fun for a Dollar

With just one dollar, you can

Plant sunflower seeds and watch them grow. If you live in an apartment, plant them in a common area to give everyone pleasure.

Take your (or a friend's) child to a candy store and buy one or two pieces of candy for you and the child. Spend lots of time choosing.

Rent a video of a classic movie.

Buy a toy or game and play with a child.

Buy a frisbee and throw it with a friend or your dog.

Go to a planetarium and see the universe.

Visit a museum or art gallery.

Ride a bus to a place you have never been.

Buy a foreign or out-of-town newspaper and see how other folks live.

Buy sequins or beads and sew or glue them on your shirt, pants, purse, socks, or shoes.

Buy a used paperback book for yourself or a friend.

Go to a garage sale and see how much you can buy for a dollar.

Buy your favorite fast food and eat it in a park, on a mountain, or by a river where you have never been before.

Give your dollar away.

What if This Were Your Last Day?

A secret to living life to the fullest is to live each day as though it was your last one on the earth. This may sound morbid but the results are transforming. Each day as you make choices about what you are going to do, ask yourself whether you would be happy with that choice if you died that night. Living from this perspective gives each day new meaning and delight.

Obviously there are always some things you may not really want to do, but you do them because they enable you to do other things you want to do. The purpose of this exercise is to do as many things that you really enjoy as possible each day so that at night you will not regret what you did during the day.

Don't put off doing the things you want to do. Do them today. Paint a picture. Learn a new song or dance. Hug someone. Tell loved ones how much you care about them. Thank people who have helped you. Say you're sorry to those you have hurt. Don't leave anything important undone.

Live each day as a full circle of life so that you can go to sleep with a feeling of peace and completion.

Experience Life's Miracles

Look closely at your thumb, a flower, your child, or your pet. Observe every detail.

Spend at least ten or fifteen minutes examining the subject you have chosen. Note the colors, textures, movement, and perfection.

Could you make a thumb, flower, child, or animal?

What if none of these existed?

What have you learned from your observation?

Epilogue

I hope the Inner Exploration Process and the other exercises in this book help you on your journey to recover your true self and make your road a little easier. Sometimes you may become discouraged with your progress, as I did many times. But keep going. You will heal. The results will be well worth the effort. Always keep in mind that you know what is best for you and whatever you do will be just what you need. Someone taught me an affirmation many years ago that has helped me through difficult times: "I am divinely guided. The path I take is always the right path. I find a way where there is no way." This affirmation applies to everyone.

Trust your own process and be gentle with yourself.

References

The Inner Exploration Process and other techniques in this book are based on the latest psychological and neurobiological research on trauma and memory and how emotional and behavioral patterns are established in our minds. Among the hundreds of resources used, the most significant are

American Psychiatric Association. 1994. *Diagnostic and Statistical Manual of Mental Disorders,* Washington, D.C.

Baron, R. A. 1992. *Psychology,* 2d ed. Boston: Allyn and Bacon.

Beahrs, J. D. 1983. Co-consciousness: A common denominator in hypnosis, multiple personality, and normalcy. *American Journal of Clinical Hypnosis* 26(2):100–113.

Benson, H. 1976. *The Relaxation Response.* New York: Avon.

Berne, E. 1961. *Transactional Analysis in Psychotherapy.* New York; Grove Press.

Bliss, E .L. 1986. *Multiple Personality, Allied Disorders and Hypnosis.* New York: Oxford.

_____. 1980. Multiple personalities: A report of fourteen cases with implications for schizophrenia and hysteria. *Archives of General Psychiatry.* 37(12):1388–1397.

Bloch, J. P. 1991. *Assessment and Treatment of Multiple Personality and Dissociative Disorders.* Sarasota, Fla.: Professional Resource Exchange.

———. 1989. Treatment of multiple personality and dissociative disorder. In *Innovations in Clinical Practice: A Source Book,* vol. 8, edited by P. A. Keller and S. R. Heyman, Sarasota, Fla.: Professional Resource Exchange.

Borysenko, J. 1990. *Guilt Is the Lesson; Love Is the Teacher.* New York: Warner Books.

———. 1987. *Minding the Body, Mending the Mind.* Boston: Addison-Wesley Publishing Co.

Braun, B. G., ed. 1986. *Treatment of Multiple Personality Disorder.* Washington, D.C.: American Psychiatric Press.

———. 1984. Hypnosis creates multiple personality: myth or reality? *International Journal of Clinical & Experimental Hypnosis.* 32(2):191–197.

Brende, J. O. 1987. Dissociative disorders in Vietnam and combat veterans. *Journal of Contemporary Psychology,* 17:77–86.

Carey-Smith, M. J. 1984. Effects of prenatal influences on later life. *New Zealand Medical Journal.* 97:13–7, 15–17.

Chamberlain, D. B. 1994. How prenatal and perinatal psychology can transform the world. *Pre- and Perinatal Psychology Journal.* 8(3)187–199.

Christos, G. A. 1995. Infant dreaming and fetal memory: a possible explanation of sudden infant death syndrome. *Medical Hypotheses* 44(4):243–250.

Corey, G. 1986. *Theory and Practice of Counseling and Psychotherapy,* 3d ed. Monterey, Calif.: Brooks/Cole Publishing Co.

Dennison, P. E. 1981. *Switching On: The Holistic Answer to Dyslexia.* Glendale, Calif.: Edu-Kinesthetics, Inc.

Dolan, Y. M. 1991. *Resolving Sexual Abuse: Solution-Focused Therapy and Ericksonian Hypnosis for Adult Survivors.* New York: W. W. Norton and Co.

Dossey, L. 1898. *Recovering the Soul.* New York: Bantam Books.

Ewin, D. E. 1994. Many memories retrieved with hypnosis are accurate. *American Journal of Clinical Hypnosis* 36(3):174–176.

Falconer, R. et al. eds,. 1995. *Trauma, Amnesia and the Denial of Abuse.* Tyler, Texas: FVSAI.

Finkelhor, D. 1986. *A Sourcebook on Child Sexual Abuse.* Thousand Oaks, Calif.: Sage Publications.

_____. 1984. *Child Sexual Abuse.* New York: Macmillan, Inc.

Finney, L. D. 1995. *Reach for Joy: How to Find the Right Therapist and Therapy for You.* Freedom, Calif.: The Crossing Press.

_____. 1992. *Reach for the Rainbow: Advanced Healing for Survivors of Sexual Abuse.* New York: Putnam Publishing Group.

Gendlin, E. T. 1981. *Focusing.* New York: Bantam.

Grof, S. with H. Z. Bennett. 1992. *The Holotropic Mind: The Three Levels of Consciousness and How They Shape Our Lives.* San Francisco: Harper-SanFrancisco.

Haley, J., 1967. *Advanced Techniques of Hypnosis and Therapy; Selected Papers of Milton H. Erickson, M.D.* Orlando, Fla.: Grune & Stratton, Inc.

Hay, L. 1987. *You Can Heal Your Life.* Santa Monica, Calif.: Hay House.

Herman, J. L. 1992. *Trauma and Recovery.* New York: HarperCollins. (Dr. Herman, a psychiatrist and Associate Clinical Professor at Harvard Medical School, has authored many significant articles in medical and psychiatric journals on the effects and treatment of trauma.)

Herman, J. L. and B. A. van der Kolk. 1987. Traumatic antecedents of borderline personality disorder. In *Psychological Trauma,* edited by B.A. van der Kolk. 111–126.

Kardiner, A. 1941. *The Traumatic Neurosis of War.* New York: P. B. Hoeber.

Kennedy-Caldwell, C. 1989. Pain in infancy. *Journal of Neuroscience Nursing* 21(6):386–388.

Kluft, R. P. 1986. Preliminary observations on age regression in multiple personality disorder patients before and after integration. *American Journal of Clinical Hypnosis* 28(3):147–156.

Kluft, R. P. 1987. An update on multiple personality disorder. *Hospital and Community Psychiatry* 38(4):363–373.

Marchal, C., et al. 1989. Naissance traumatique, memoire precoce et structuration de l'image de soi: Approche a l'aide du test des contes. *Archives de Psychologie* 57(222):195–214.

Moscovitch, M. 1985. Memory from infancy to old age: implications for theories of normal and pathological memory. *Annals New York Academy of Sciences* 444:78–96.

Fedor-Freyberg, P., et al. eds. 1988. *Prenatal and Perinatal Psychology and Medicine.* Pearl River, N.Y.: The Parthenon Publishing Group.

Rama, S. 1978. *Freedom from the Bondage of Karma.* Penn: The Himalayan International Institute of Yoga Science.

Riedlinger, T., et al. 1986. Taking birth trauma seriously. *Medical Hypotheses* 19(1):15–25.

Ross, C. A., and G. Anderson. 1988. Phenomenological overlap of multiple personality disorder and obsessive-compulsive disorder. *The Journal of Nervous and Mental Disease* 176:295–298.

Rossi, E. L. 1986. *The Psychobiology of Mind-Body Healing: New Concepts of Therapeutic Hypnosis.* New York: W. W. Norton and Co.

Rossi, E. L., with D. Nimmons. 1991. *The 20 Minute Break: Using the New Science of Ultradian Rhythms.* Los Angeles: Jeremy P. Tarcher, Inc.

Rowan, J. 1990. *Subpersonalities: The People Inside Us.* New York: Routledge.

Schwartz, R. 1987. Our Multiple Selves. *Networker,* March-April, 25, 27.

Terr, L. 1994. *Unchained Memories: True Stories of Traumatic Memories, Lost and Found.* New York: Basic Books.

Van der Kolk, B. A., et al. 1996. *Traumatic Stress: Human Adaptations to Overwhelming Experience.* New York: Guilford Press. (Dr. van der Kolk, a psychiatrist on the faculty at Harvard Medical School and coprincipal investigator for the American Psychiatric Association on PTSD, is recognized as one of the foremost experts on the effects of trauma.)

Van der Kolk, B. A., et al. 1991. The intrusive past: the flexibility of memory and the engraving of trauma. *American Imago* 48(4): 425–454.

Van der Kolk, B. A. 1995. Dissociation and defragmentary nature of traumatic memory. *Journal of Traumatic Stress.* October.

———. 1988. The trauma spectrum: the interaction of biological and social events in the genesis of the trauma response. *Journal of Traumatic Stress* 1:273–286.

Wender, P., et al. 1982. *Mind, Mood and Medicine.* New York: New American Library.

Whitfield, L. 1995. *Memory and Abuse; Remembering and Healing the Effects of Trauma.* Deerfield Beach, Florida: Health Communications, Inc.

Wilbur, C. B. 1984. Treatment of multiple personality. *Psychiatric Annals* 14(1):27–31.

Resources

Addiction Alternatives (Rational Recovery)
    1851 East First Street, Suite 820
    Santa Ana, CA 92705
    (714) 550-9311

Adult Children of Alcoholics Central Service Board and Interim World
    Service Organization
    P.O. Box 3216
    Torrance, CA 90510
    (310) 534-1815

Al-Anon/Alateen Family Group Headquarters
    1600 Corporate Landing Parkway
    Virginia Beach, VA 23454-5617
    (757) 563-1600

Alcoholics Anonymous (AA)
    475 Riverside Drive
    P.O. Box 459
    Grand Central Station, NY 10164
Check your phone directory first for local meetings.

American Humane Association
    American Association for Protecting Children
    63 Inverness Drive E
    Englewood, CO 80112-5117
    (303) 792-9900
    (800) 227-5242
Provides professional publications and fields public inquiries regarding child protective services and child abuse and neglect.

American Self-Help Clearinghouse
    St. Clares-Riverside Medical Center
    25 Pocano
    Denville, NJ 07834
    (201) 625-7101
    TDD (201) 625-9053 (for hearing impaired)
Provides a directory of U.S. and Canadian self-help organizations and literature for starting support groups.

Anxiety Disorders Association of America
    11900 Parklawn Drive, Suite 100
    Rockville, MD 20852-2624
    (301) 231-8368

Childhelp USA
    P.O. Box 630
    Los Angeles, CA 90028
    Hotline: (800) 4-A-CHILD or
    (800) 422-4453
Provides twenty-four-hour crisis counseling by mental health professionals. Serves adult and child victims of child abuse and neglect, offenders, and parents who are fearful of abusing or who want information on effective parenting.

Incest Survivors Anonymous World Service Office
    P.O. Box 17245
    Long Beach, CA 90807-7245
    (310) 428-5599
A nonprofit organization of local support groups based on the twelve-step program. Check your phone directory first for local meetings.

National Committee for Prevention of Child Abuse
    332 South Michigan Avenue, Suite 1600
    Chicago, IL 606604-4357
    (312) 663-3520

Sixty-eight local chapters throughout the fifty states. Provides information and statistics on child abuse and maintains an extensive publications list. The National Research Center provides information for professionals on programs, methods for evaluating programs, and research findings.

National Council on Child Abuse and Family Violence
    1155 Connecticut Avenue, Suite 400
    Washington, DC 20036
    (202) 429-6695

Provides personal safety curricula, including child abuse and neglect prevention for school children and model prevention programs for adolescents. Educational materials for parents, children, and community groups are available.

National Crime Prevention Council
    1700 K Street, NW
    2nd Floor
    Washington, DC 20006
    (202) 466-6272

National Exchange Club Foundation for Prevention of Child Abuse
    3050 Central Avenue
    Toledo, OH 43606
    (419) 535-3232

Provides parent aid services to abusive and neglecting families in thirty-seven cities.

Parents United/Daughters and Sons United/Adults Molested as
    Children United
    232 East Gish Road
    San Jose, CA 95112
    (408) 453-7616

One hundred fifty chapters nationwide. Provides guided self-help for sexually abusive parents as well as child and adult victims of sexual abuse.

The Sidran Foundation
    2328 West Joppa Road, Suite 15
    Lutherville, MD 21093
    (410) 825-8888

A nonprofit educational and research foundation focusing on catastrophic trauma in childhood. Maintains database of support groups, treatment providers, and organizations by state.

Spiritual Emergence Network
    The Institute of Transpersonal Psychology
    250 Oak Grove Avenue
    Menlo Park, CA 94025
    (415) 493-4430

Founded by Christina Grof in 1980, this network helps people understand and find appropriate help for crisis states during the transformational process. Refers to local therapists. It is wise to check these recommendations and obtain a second opinion.

Trauma, a bimonthly publication of Survivors and Victims Empowered
    P.O. Box 3030
    Lancaster, PA 17604-3030

An excellent, readable resource for recent developments and practical applications about trauma abuse survivorship, therapy, and related subjects.

About Lynne D. Finney, J.D., M.S.W.

Lynne Finney is an author, lecturer, and former lawyer and psychotherapist specializing in the treatment of childhood trauma and helping people live more fulfilling lives. Lynne has also been a diplomat, United Nations policy advisor to the Agency for International Development, and was appointed by President Carter's administration as a director of a federal banking agency. She served on White House task forces, was counsel to a U.S. Senator, and has been a law professor in Washington, D.C., California, and Utah. She was also an attorney-investigator on the House of Representatives Special Subcommittee on Investigations (the subcommittee was portrayed in the movie *Quiz Show*).

Lynne has appeared on over one hundred radio and television shows throughout the United States and Canada, including three times on Larry King's shows. She trains therapists in the United States and Canada and teaches at a college.

Her first book, *Reach for the Rainbow: Advanced Healing for Survivors of Sexual Abuse,* won an award for research from the National Association of Social Workers and is now in its second edition. Her second book, *Reach for Joy: How to Find the Right Therapist and Therapy for You,* was released in 1995, and she is presently working on a book about millennium fears.

As a child, Lynne was physically and sexually abused by her father, an award-winning novelist and screenwriter. She developed the techniques for psychological and spiritual healing in this book as a result of her personal healing journey as well as through years of research and working with clients as a therapist.

If you would like more information about Lynne's lectures and workshops, you may order a two-cassette audiotape package of her lectures entitled *Clearing Your Past,* from Sounds True. These include a discussion of the Inner Exploration Process, a guided meditation for compassion and spiritual growth, information about how selective perception creates out reality, how to change our perceptions, and much more. To order call 1-800-333-9185, or write to Sounds True, P.O. Box 8010, Boulder, CO 80306-8010.

For information about Lynne's lectures and workshops, please write to Lynne Finney, P.O. Box 681539, Park City, UT 84068-1539.

More New Harbinger Titles for Personal Growth and Change

THE POWER OF FOCUSING

Focusing teacher and innovator Anne Weiser Cornell takes you through a process of listening to your body and letting the messages that emerge lead to insights, decisions, and positive change. "An invaluable tool for serious students of the inner life." —Helen Palmer.

Item POF Paperback, $12.95

ILLUMINATING THE HEART

Authors Greg and Barbara Markway outline nine essential steps that couples can take to examine their spiritual beliefs, search for shared meaning and purpose, and reconnect to each other and the wider community.

Item LUM Paperback, $13.95

HYPNOSIS FOR CHANGE

Now in its third edition, this classic guide shows you how to use self-hypnosis to harness your natural abilities to relax, ease pain, heal, and change.

Item HYP3 Paperback, $13.95

VISUALIZATION FOR CHANGE

The updated second edition offers a more practical, step-by-step approach than most other books on the use of imagery for self-improvement and healing.

Item VIS2 Paperback, $13.95

THE THREE MINUTE MEDITATOR

The expanded third edition offers a down-to-earth introduction to the basics of using meditation to unwind your mind, cope with the stresses of daily life, and treat yourself to the powerful benefits of self-acceptance and inner peace.

Item MED3 Paperback, $12.95

THE ADDICTION WORKBOOK

Explains the facts about addiction and provides simple, step-by-step directions for working through the stages of the quitting process.

Item AWB Paperback, $17.95

Call **toll-free 1-800-748-6273** to order. Have your Visa or Mastercard number ready. Or send a check for the titles you want to New Harbinger Publications, 5674 Shattuck Avenue, Oakland, CA 94609. Include $3.80 for the first book and 75¢ for each additional book to cover shipping and handling. (California residents please include appropriate sales tax.) Allow four to six weeks for delivery.

Prices subject to change without notice.

Other New Harbinger Self-Help Titles

Preparing for Surgery, $17.95
Coming Out Everyday, $13.95
Ten Things Every Parent Needs to Know, $12.95
The Power of Two, $12.95
It's Not OK Anymore, $13.95
The Daily Relaxer, $12.95
The Body Image Workbook, $17.95
Living with ADD, $17.95
Taking the Anxiety Out of Taking Tests, $12.95
The Taking Charge of Menopause Workbook, $17.95
Living with Angina, $12.95
PMS: Women Tell Women How to Control Premenstrual Syndrome, $13.95
Five Weeks to Healing Stress: The Wellness Option, $17.95
Choosing to Live: How to Defeat Suicide Through Cognitive Therapy, $12.95
Why Children Misbehave and What to Do About It, $14.95
Illuminating the Heart, $13.95
When Anger Hurts Your Kids, $12.95
The Addiction Workbook, $17.95
The Mother's Survival Guide to Recovery, $12.95
The Chronic Pain Control Workbook, Second Edition, $17.95
Fibromyalgia & Chronic Myofascial Pain Syndrome, $19.95
Diagnosis and Treatment of Sociopaths, $44.95
Flying Without Fear, $12.95
Kid Cooperation: How to Stop Yelling, Nagging & Pleading and Get Kids to Cooperate, $12.95
The Stop Smoking Workbook: Your Guide to Healthy Quitting, $17.95
Conquering Carpal Tunnel Syndrome and Other Repetitive Strain Injuries, $17.95
The Tao of Conversation, $12.95
Wellness at Work: Building Resilience for Job Stress, $17.95
What Your Doctor Can't Tell You About Cosmetic Surgery, $13.95
An End to Panic: Breakthrough Techniques for Overcoming Panic Disorder, $17.95
On the Clients Path: A Manual for the Practice of Solution-Focused Therapy, $39.95
Living Without Procrastination: How to Stop Postponing Your Life, $12.95
Goodbye Mother, Hello Woman: Reweaving the Daughter Mother Relationship, $14.95
Letting Go of Anger: The 10 Most Common Anger Styles and What to Do About Them, $12.95
Messages: The Communication Skills Workbook, Second Edition, $13.95
Coping With Chronic Fatigue Syndrome: Nine Things You Can Do, $12.95
The Anxiety & Phobia Workbook, Second Edition, $17.95
Thueson's Guide to Over-the-Counter Drugs, $13.95
Natural Women's Health: A Guide to Healthy Living for Women of Any Age, $13.95
I'd Rather Be Married: Finding Your Future Spouse, $13.95
The Relaxation & Stress Reduction Workbook, Fourth Edition, $17.95
Living Without Depression & Manic Depression: A Workbook for Maintaining Mood Stability, $17.95
Coping With Schizophrenia: A Guide For Families, $13.95
Visualization for Change, Second Edition, $13.95
Postpartum Survival Guide, $13.95
Angry All the Time: An Emergency Guide to Anger Control, $12.95
Couple Skills: Making Your Relationship Work, $13.95
Handbook of Clinical Psychopharmacology for Therapists, $39.95
Weight Loss Through Persistence, $13.95
Post-Traumatic Stress Disorder: A Complete Treatment Guide, $39.95
Stepfamily Realities: How to Overcome Difficulties and Have a Happy Family, $13.95
The Chemotherapy Survival Guide, $11.95
The Deadly Diet, Second Edition: Recovering from Anorexia & Bulimia, $13.95
Last Touch: Preparing for a Parent's Death, $11.95
Self-Esteem, Second Edition, $13.95
I Can't Get Over It, A Handbook for Trauma Survivors, Second Edition, $15.95
Concerned Intervention, When Your Loved One Won't Quit Alcohol or Drugs, $12.95
Dying of Embarrassment: Help for Social Anxiety and Social Phobia, $12.95
The Depression Workbook: Living With Depression and Manic Depression, $17.95
Prisoners of Belief: Exposing & Changing Beliefs that Control Your Life, $12.95
Men & Grief: A Guide for Men Surviving the Death of a Loved One, $13.95
When the Bough Breaks: A Helping Guide for Parents of Sexually Abused Children, $11.95
When Once Is Not Enough: Help for Obsessive Compulsives, $13.95
The Three Minute Meditator, Third Edition, $12.95
Beyond Grief: A Guide for Recovering from the Death of a Loved One, $13.95
Leader's Guide to the Relaxation & Stress Reduction Workbook, Fourth Edition, $19.95
The Divorce Book, $13.95
Hypnosis for Change: A Manual of Proven Techniques, Third Edition, $13.95
When Anger Hurts, $13.95
Lifetime Weight Control, $12.95

Call **toll free, 1-800-748-6273,** to order. Have your Visa or Mastercard number ready. Or send a check for the titles you want to New Harbinger Publications, Inc., 5674 Shattuck Ave., Oakland, CA 94609. Include $3.80 for the first book and 75¢ for each additional book, to cover shipping and handling. (California residents please include appropriate sales tax.) Allow four to six weeks for delivery.

Prices subject to change without notice.